the Quest for the Galloping hogan

the Quest for the Galloping hogan

by Matthew J. Culligan-Hogan

CROWN PUBLISHERS, INC.
New York

Inquiries should be addressed to Crown Publishers, Inc., One Park Avenue, New York, N.Y. 10016

Printed in the United States of America
Published simultaneously in Canada by
General Publishing Company Limited

Library of Congress Cataloging in Publication Data

Culligan, Matthew J 1918-
The Quest for the Galloping Hogan

1. Hogan family. 2. Ireland—History—1691- 3. Culligan, Matthew J., 1918-
4. Ireland—
Genealogy. I. Title.

CS499.H57 1979   929'.2'09415   78-27642

ISBN 0-517-53665-X

Book design: Shari de Miskey

Dedicated to the Wild Geese of Ireland

War-battered dogs we are,
    Fighters in every clime;
Fillers of trenches and graves,
    Mockers be-mocked by time;
War-dogs, hungry and grey,
    Gnawing a naked bone
Fighters in every clime,
    Every cause but our own.

EMILY LAWLESS,
"With the Wild Geese"

Those gentlemen of Ireland, who, with all
the disadvantages of being exiles and strangers
have been able to distinguish themselves in
so many parts of Europe by their valor and
conduct above all other nations . . .

JONATHAN SWIFT

Oh the dreaming, dreaming, the torturing,
heart-scalding, never satisfying,
dreaming, dreaming, dreaming . . .

G. B. SHAW,

John Bull's Other Island

Contents

Acknowledgments

I am deeply indebted to Nat Wartels, the founder and builder of Crown Publishers. His help with the "editorial architecture" and his continuing encouragement have been invaluable. Putting this manuscript and me in the hands of Crown editor Pat Winsor was generalship of the highest order.

I am most grateful for the contribution made by a copy editor trained in Irish culture and history, Catherine Riley.

Judith Valentine re-created the Rapparee's hat which adorns the cover, and cheered me through a half-dozen rewrites.

Ed Rose translated the ancient Portuguese as only a most scholarly Portuguese gentleman could.

Liam Hogan took the photographs that portray parts of Sarsfield's Ride.

Le Comte Patrick de MacMahon opened the way for me at the Bibliothèque Nationale, at Vincennes, securing the critical documents about the Hogans in the flight of the Wild Geese.

The late, great Norman Rockwell painted the portrait on the back cover.

Three lines from "September 1913" are reprinted by permission of Macmillan Publishing Company, Inc., from *Collected Poems of William Butler Yeats.* Copyright 1916 by Macmillan Publishing Company, Inc. Renewed 1944 by Bertha Georgie Yeats.

Prologue

IRELAND IS a country with an astonishing past, a dreadful present, and a potentially great future.

The culture of ancient Ireland is somewhat analogous to three others, of which there is substantial, though mute, evidence. They are the Mayan, Incan, and Aztec cultures.

The Incan and Aztec cultures were impacted by the Spanish military-religious empire and ruthlessly destroyed. The disappearance of the Mayans is still a mystery. Ireland was first settled by the Milesians of the Iberian peninsula and later by the Celts of central Europe. It was then invaded by the Vikings and Normans, whom Ireland absorbed. It was later smothered by the Tudor English military-religious empire. Ireland was not destroyed, but it has been treated to almost a thousand years of a peculiar kind of agony, which I call *cultricide*, the killing of a culture. The ultimate torture was the "designed frightfulness" of Oliver Cromwell in the middle of the seventeenth century. Cromwell described it as "a useful terror."

The Quest for the Galloping Hogan is not a history, nor is it a glorification of Ireland. It is rather a presentation of a case for Ireland to Irish men and women and to those who are horrified, deeply concerned, and confused by the bombings, burnings, and shootings in the north of Ireland. It is a shout of rage over the attempted murder of the human spirit. It is the search for the quintessential spirit of the indestructible, and

1

sometimes intractable, Irish.

Like an Irishman's answer—always a question—I make my case by indirection, in a narrative about one side of my family, the Hogans of County Clare. My mother was Sarah Hogan, one of eleven girls born to Domenic Hogan of Scariff.

It was the inspirational and strangely beautiful death of my mother, at seventy-eight, that gave rise to the first thoughts about this book. She collapsed while awaiting her beloved tea, murmuring, "Jesus, Mary, and Joseph, help me." The plea, heard by her eldest daughter, my sister Marie, was said without fear or pain. Every night of her life she had repeated that little prayer. Little wonder that when she felt the dread change that she would ask for their help. Eight hours after the mass cerebral hemorrhage, from which she never regained consciousness, her friends came and took her softly away.

After the funeral mass, her children, grandchildren, sons-in-law and daughters-in-law followed her casket up the aisle, bawling like children. I concluded that this superior lady should be known by many more than her children and friends.

Later, another reason for the book rudely intruded, the moment I finished reading the astoundingly successful *Trinity* written by Leon Uris. The final paragraph

> When all of this [the Easter Rebellion of 1916] was done, a republic eventually came to pass, but the troubles and sorrows have never left that tragic lovely land. For you see, in Ireland there is no future, only the past happening over and over.

sent me into a smoking rage. Most irritating was the fact that Leon Uris, a Jew who should have known how much the Jews and Irish have in common, particularly about freedom, committed the deadliest of the seven deadly sins—despair. His previous success, *Exodus*, which glorified the heroic struggle of the Jews in their homeland was a message of hope. But *Trinity*, the book read by more people than all the other books about Ireland published during the last two decades, ended with a dangerous slander. If many native Irish men and women and children believe Ireland has no future—only the past happening over and over—then it will not. But I know, after five years of intensive research in Ireland, France, Portugal, and the Vatican in Rome, that unquenchable hope, which makes all things possible, is a fundamental part of the quintessential spirit of the Irish.

Other reasons for this book began to surface rapidly.

One was a kind of demand impulse, a transfer of imagery a decade old. The mental picture was of two men, less than five years apart in age, meeting and talking in a nearly oval office in Washington, D.C.

One, who sat in a rocking chair, was the President of the United States, the late John Fitzgerald Kennedy. The other, president of a $600,000,000 publishing empire, The Curtis Publishing Company, was myself. The meeting and conversation were unique. Here were two descendants of Irish immigrants meeting in the office of the most powerful figure in the world.

More astoundingly, the ancient map of Ireland, which showed the general locations of the Dalcassian clans of what is now Tipperary, Limerick, and Clare, disclosed that the Clan O'Kennedy lands were contiguous to the O'Hogan lands. I did not then know the terrible truth of Lorrha, the bitter fruit of an internacine battle between the two families. (The terrible truth of Lorrha is described in Chapter 5.)

Northern Ireland is the only place in the English-speaking world in which there is still terrorist killing, maiming, and destruction. It is an unacceptable outrage, which *must* be stopped and *can* be stopped by hope and positive action.

President John F. Kennedy confided in Pierre Salinger, as his sentimental journey to Ireland came to a close, that he saw a role for Ireland as a bridge between the Third World countries and the industrial democracies. This prospective service to the world could come about because of the excellent, fair, and objective performances of Irish members of the United Nations peace missions to the Congo, Cypress, and the Near East. Ireland can better fulfill this role when it solves its problems in the North.

The Republic of Ireland, encompassing six-sevenths of the land, is a new democracy in a world in which the tide has been running against democratic governments. Ireland, Israel, democratized Spain, restored Portugal, and India may have reversed the tide.

The Hogans are a microcosm of the basic native Irish, those who descended from the Dalcassian clans. As such, they are an important clue to the quintessential spirit of the Irish.

I appeal to a higher power in establishing the background of the Clan Hogan. My source is MacLysaght's *Irish Families: Their Names, Arms and*

Origins, first published in the United States by Crown Publishers in 1972.

O'Hogan

The Hogans are a Dalcassian family, their eponymous ancestor being Ógan who was descended from an uncle of Brian Boru, the most cele-brated of all the Kings of Ireland. The Dalcassian territory extended well beyond the boundaries of Co. Clare which was the heart of Thomond, their country. The Hogans occupied the extreme north-eastern part of it and their chief lived at Ardcrony, near Nenagh, Co. Tipperary. The name is numerous in Ireland, being among the hundred commonest sur-names. The great majority of the eight thousand or so persons so called (which is the estimate of the present Hogan population) belong to their original native habitat, being found to-day in Counties Tipperary, Clare and Limerick. . . . One of the minor Corca Laidhe septs was O'Hogan. In Irish the name is Ó hÓgáin but the prefix O is only occasionally met with in the modern form in English. In the seventeenth century the name was often written Ogan. There is a placename Ballyhogan in the parish of Dysart, Co. Clare.

The most famous Hogan is probably John Hogan (1800–1858), an Irish sculptor of international repute; but to Irishmen the romantic figure of "Galloping Hogan" (the date of whose birth and death I cannot trace), the hero of Sarsfield's exploit at Ballyneety (1690), makes the most ap-peal. Maurice O'Hogan was a notable Bishop: he held the see of Kildare from 1281 to 1298. Rev. Edmund Hogan, S.J. (1831–1917), did much work as an editor of manuscripts and produced his best known book *Onomasticon Gaedelicum* at the age of seventy-two. The first Minister of Agriculture in the Irish Free State Patrick Hogan (1891–1936), was one of three brothers who have distinguished themselves in various national activities in our own time.

MacLysaght's *Irish Families: Their Names, Arms and Origins* proved an initial boon, then a threat. It provided names, places, dates, and events, but if just one citation proved inaccurate, all would be questionable. There were worrisome moments, and a waste of two days looking for records on a Hogan in the wrong part of Ireland. But, ultimately, I did confirm every fact in MacLysaght's description of the O'Hogans—and more, so much more.

A LIST OF THE FAMILIES THAT MADE UP THE DALCASSIANS

Modern Name	Ancient Name	Meaning of Name
Conroy	Conray	Con the King
King	McConry	Son of Con the King
McArthur	Artureigh	The Sailor
McBrody	Brodach	Exciter
McCoghian	Coghlan	The warrior
McCormick	Cormicain	Son of the crown
McEneiry	Enrach	Solitary
McGilduff	Giolladurh	Dark boy
McGildea	Giolladea	Servant of science
McGrath	Craith	the tormented
McLysaght	O'Brien	Grandson of Eloquent
McMahon	Mainchin	Wounded hand
McNamara	Conmara	Con of the Sea
McReedy	Riada	The umpire
McTeigue	O'Brien	Grandson of Eloquent
Meade	Meadhra	Joyful
O'Brien	Brian	The author
O'Bilrigh	Bilrigh	The small king
O'Brody	Broadach	Exciter
O'Bellian	Beolach	Active soldier
O'Clanchy	Clanach	Virtue
O'Cormac	Cormicain	Son of Crown
O'Conklin	Congolaighs	The complainer
O'Dea	O'Brien	Author
O'Carmody	O'Meadhra	Joyful
O'Delany	Deaghlabhairb	Proper in Speech
O'Finnellan	Feinnedhelan	Perfect soldier
O'Gleason	Gleasain	The Tuner
O'Grady	Gradha	Noble
O'Griffin	Gribhean	The Griffin
O'Hea	Easc	Old
O'Herlighy	Erlamh	The Holy Man
O'Hennigan	Hennigan	Beholder
O'Hartigan	Earthoghadh	First choice

O'Healy	Eailamh	Nimble
O'Hurley	Uriataidh	The active
O'Hogan	Oghdha	The sincere
O'Hiffernan	Irfionnech	Wicked
O'Hickey	Hicidhes	Healer
O'Hannan	Huanan	Terrible
O'Honeen	Oineach	Generous
O'Howley	Ollamh	Doctor
O'Hanraghty	Annracht	Poet Laureate
O'Hanragman	Anraidhan	Champion
O'Kearney	Cearnach	Victorious
O'Kelleher	Ceallacher	Warrior
O'Kennedy	Ceanadh	Favoring
O'Kerwick	O'Brien	Author
O'Looney	Loinsighes	Mariner
O'Mullanny	Miollaineach	Thoughtful
O'Mullowney	Miollainneach	Thoughtful
O'Meara	Meadra	Joyful
O'Moroney	Mormheamnach	Magnanimous
O'Neaghtain	Neaghtain	Neutral
O'Quill	Cuilfhion	Fairhaired
O'Quinn	Cuingidh	Hero
O'Regan	Raegha	A choice
O'Riady	Ryada	Umpire
O'Scully	O'Brien	Hospitable
O'Slattery	O'Brien	The killer
O'Sexon	Seasnain	A defense
O'Spillane	Speoilain	Acute
O'Shanaghan	Siansanach	Resounding
O'Shine	Siodhachain	Sprightly
O'Tuohy	O'Brien	Author
O'Teigue	Teigue	Covering
O'Tuomy	Tuama	Fierce

In particular, I confirmed the view of the esteemed historian William Edward Lecky, who said of the exiled Irish, "How large a portion of [their] energy and ability [was spent] in foreign lands, and ruinous must have been the consequences at home."

His use of the word *ruinous* was apt, for in the late 1800s Ireland was truly a ruin. Its survival, with its native Irish culture intact, is a victory of the human spirit to which only the survival of European Jews during World War II is comparable. Regarding the "energy and ability" of the Irish in foreign lands, Lecky was doubly right.

By the beginning of the nineteenth century the Irish all over the Western World were highly visible, respected, and influential in politics, engineering, architecture, art, educational and societal fields. But, except for a few patriots, the native Irish in Ireland, bled white by exile and emigration, exhausted by lost rebellions every fifty years, were barely alive as a distinct, ancient culture. Not until 1916, in the "glorious folly" of the Easter Rebellion, did the spirit of the Irish flare brightly again—and within six years the Irish in sixth-sevenths of the island would be free. Unquenchable hope had made it possible.

The final piece in the mosaic of my search for the ancestry of the name Hogan finally fell into place at the last stage of preparation for production of this book.

My benefactor in the case of Ógan, "their eponymous ancestor . . . who was descended from an uncle of Brian Boru," was Colonel Sean O'Driscoll, an American of Irish descent living now in Ireland.

Colonel O'Driscoll was chief gunnery officer of the U.S. Eighth Air Force during World War II. With a fine sense of history, he acquired and completely restored Castle Matrix, in Rathkeal, in County Limerick, Ireland. Over two decades he amassed an extraordinary library of manuscripts, sketches, engravings, monographs, and books about ancient Ireland. It took O'Driscoll over a year to discover the identity of Ógan and his forebears.

The king of the Dalcassians in A.D. 942 was Lorcan, called Fingin. He had four sons: Congal, Cineadh, Cosgragh, and Lonargan. Cosgragh had a son named Aither, and he was the father of Ógan, who started the Clan Ógan/O'Hogan/Hogan around A.D. 1050.

There were towering barriers to my discovery of the Galloping Hogan when I started the quest in 1974. In fact, it would have been impossible except for these characteristics of Ireland and the Irish:

Ireland became an island toward the end of the Ice Age, about 6000 B.C.

A long, continuous famine drove an expeditionary force of Iberians to what their chief Druid described as the "Island of Destiny," Innisfail.

The favorable report of the expeditionary force started a mass migration of Iberians to Innisfail, who then called themselves Milesians. This was probably sometime around 500 B.C.

The Milesians settled in what was called, in ancient times, Dalcassia, now comprised of the modern counties of Clare, Limerick and Tipperary, in central western Ireland.

Around 300 B.C. the Gallo-Celts of Central Europe migrated to Ireland. They, the Milesians, and the almost legendary earlier races, mingled to become the basic native Irish stock.

The Romans invaded Europe, leaving excellent written documents of the Celts in Europe.

The basic native Irish adopted Brehon Law, two principal features of which were: land ownership by clans, and clan leadership by election, the leadership being restricted to specific clans.

Record-keeping was a sacred duty of the clans. Therefore, heavy penalties were given for failure or falsification.

Farmlands, forests, mountains, and bogs were scattered throughout Ireland, making natural, logical and peaceful divisions of the clans.

The conversion of Ireland to Christianity by Saint Patrick and others around A.D. 500 added written records to the oral and archeological records that extended back to approximately 4000 B.C.

Monks in monasteries copied original documents, sending many to the Vatican in Rome. These and some others escaped the burning and destruction of the Viking invasions.

The Normans came in waves starting in the twelfth century, bringing new architectural, technical and administrative skills.

The native Irish and Normans mingled through gossiprage, fosterage, and intermarriage.

Anglo-Saxon Catholics, accepted as coreligionists, settled in Ireland during the twelfth through the fourteenth centuries.

A combination of those circumstances made Ireland and the native Catholic Irish what they were. Then—starting in the seventeenth century—into that Ireland and that people came what the Irish considered the *foreign* influence—English, Scottish, and Welsh soldiers and settlers.

They came in waves in the wake of Cromwell's religious war in Ireland, and some of the so-called aristocracy who came as leeches behaved in a manner that was a disgrace to the aristocracy of Europe. They deserved the appellation "the slutten aristocracy," as they were to become known. But it must be remembered that this slutten aristocracy was as brutal and rapacious in England and Scotland as it was in Ireland.

They were an embarrassment to the great English race for whom this author has a limitless affection and respect that commenced on the decks of the H.M.S. *Brittanic* during a sixteen-day convoy trip to Liverpool in England. I accidentally found the niche in which the English officers took their topside breaks. Their desperate courage, good humor, and basic decency were qualities I was to find all over England during the months I served there, while awaiting shipment to France.

It has become all too facile for the adult world to forget what a great race the English were and are as the press parrots the litany of their dōmestic problems. The English people were betrayed too often by their aristocracy.

The phrase *slutten aristocracy* was coined in the Crimea by Lawrence Godkin, an Irishman who was the second great war correspondent, in that branch of journalism spawned during the Crimean War. (The first was another Irishman, William Howard Russell. He gained immortality within the profession by inventing the description that was to capture the fancy of all. "I am," he said, "the miserable parent of a luckless tribe.")

Lawrence Godkin was so sickened and outraged by the sloth, inefficiency, and indifferent brutality of the English officers, whose men were dying of hunger, neglect, and disease, that he wrote reports for the *Times* of London seldom matched anywhere for their abrasiveness.

1 🍀 The Clan Hogan

In Valor's Morn or Sorrow's Night
To that pure Gem of Nature: freedom.

ANCIENT DALCASSIAN POEM,
favorite of Domenic Hogan, Fenian

THE FIRST Hogan destined to become a folk hero was honored with the sobriquet the "Galloping Hogan." A *gallop*, from the older *wallop*, was a measure of distance in ancient Gaelic. Only the greatest horseman in each generation could earn this rarely given title for his skill and daring.

Other bona fide Irish folk heroes of the seventeenth century were Patrick Sarsfield of County Limerick, the earl of Lucan, and Mahon, a cousin of the Galloping Hogan who did not have much visibility in Ireland, but came into his own in France. Mahon and Hogan had a common ancestor—Lorcan, King of the Dalcassians, who died in A.D. 924.

The exploits of Patrick Sarsfield are more historically evident. His family ruled their lands for 500 years before his birth. The first Sarsfield was Thomas de Saresfield, who came to Ireland with the Normans. He stayed, the name became Sarsfield, and, with intermarriage, the Sarsfields became "more Irish than the Irish," as the saying goes.

Patrick Sarsfield and the Galloping Hogan were close friends and fierce allies. They are, in fact, the sole surviving heroes of the so-called Jacobite War of 1690–1691, which featured the deposed King James II "leading" the native Irish in a fight against King William of Orange, who succeeded James as ruler of England.

King James was certainly no hero. He became the butt of ridicule known to every Irish schoolboy. When he arrived in Dublin after the decimation and defeat of his army in the Battle of the Boyne in 1690, he complained that "the cowards ran." His hostess, not a Churchill for nothing, replied, "Yes, your Grace, and *you* won the race."

This book is an account of my search for the Galloping Hogan, who left Ireland in exile with Sarsfield and most of his troops—becoming one of the legendary, heroic, and often tragic wanderers called the Wild Geese—as part of the tradeoff for the Treaty of Limerick, signed with the representatives of King William in 1691. Several thousand Irish, including Hogan, Sarsfield, and Mahon, agreed to permanent exile as a feature of the treaty, which in other respects was remarkable for its tolerance.

The most widely known and easiest to trace of the wanderers was Patrick Sarsfield. Portraits and statues of him exist. Mahon became a marshal of France and started the line that gave France the second president of the Third Republic, Le Duc de Magenta, Marshal Mac-Mahon.

However, when I started my quest for the Galloping Hogan in 1974, I found almost nothing beyond ballads, legends, and a hideaway in County Clare still known as Hogan's Glen. It drove me to musty archives, libraries, and historical societies in America, France, Portugal, Italy, and, of course, Ireland.

I suppose in my psyche I knew all along that the search for the Galloping Hogan would turn out to be a search for the spirit of the Clan Hogan, the native Irish, and myself. What answers there were had to be found, if at all, in genetics, racial memory, life experiences, and other forces in that darkest yet brightest of all places, the mind and spirit of us all.

I couldn't have been more than six or seven when I noticed that schoolmates and friends mentioned grandfathers and grandmothers, first in relation to Christmas presents. I was upset because I didn't have any—grandparents *or* Christmas presents from them. My mother then told me that her father had died in 1907 in Ireland and her mother nine years later.

This sketchy family history did not at all satisfy me. My mother then told me my grandfather was a leader in the fight for Irish freedom. That cheered me. Then she sent me off happy by telling me about our heroic ancestor, the Galloping Hogan. It might have left a fleeting impression except for the word "galloping." At that stage of my young life, I loved horses. My life was enriched by the presence of the New York Mounted Police Academy less than a mile from where we lived in Washington Heights. I haunted the place and later volunteered to work around the stable as a groom in exchange for a chance to exercise the horses. Most of the mounted police were young Irishmen, many without families. They seemed happy to adopt me as a mascot. I learned to ride, not formfully, but competently. The Galloping Hogan became an idol to me then.

Many years later, when I was in my early thirties, the great event for my mother was her first trip back to Ireland. I remember so well the bon voyage party on the beautiful new liner, *United States*. All the years and constant pain of arthritis seemed to drop away as she laughed, and even danced a bit.

At our first dinner after she returned, she told us of the bittersweetness of her visit. And for the first time we talked about her father, Domenic Hogan. I recall Mother saying, "He wasn't around much when I was a girl—always off somewhere on Fenian business. But when he was home, he was grand."

She remembered he would often ride in at night, exhausted, but in the morning he'd be up with the thirteen children for breakfast. "Then we'd all walk from the house to the village center, waving to the villagers, most of whom were relatives."

I asked what he looked like. She described him with an old Irishism: "He was a fine figure of a man." She said he was tall when he stood, but that he walked with difficulty. He had been wounded, she knew, in 1867, in a seemingly futile uprising called the Land Reform.

When I asked how she knew, she triumphantly brought forth a sheaf of resolutions she had found in her deceased mother's papers. They read:

Resolution—World Association of Claremen:
Whereas, having heard of the death, with deepest regret, of Domenic Hogan, of Scariff, County Clare, a man who gave the best part of his life to his native land, carrying to his grave physical injuries received in the battles of 1867, be it resolved that in his death Ireland has lost one of her most gallant and faithful sons.

Resolution—The Fenian Brotherhood:
On that stormy night in 1867, he joined the Fenians in the gallant

uprising in Limerick. In the last battle at Kilmallock he was seriously wounded, and carried the results to his grave.

I did some quick calculations. Domenic Hogan was wounded in 1867, born in 1840. His father was born in 1810, just a century and a quarter after the Galloping Hogan rode over the Irish countryside. Despite Domenic's wounds, he married and fathered thirteen children, two boys and eleven girls. All but three of the girls came to America. One stayed in Ireland, one went to Australia, and one went to South Africa. The daughters of Rose, who stayed in Ireland, married men named Guilfoyle and O'Beirne. I realized with a start that this was not ancient history— Domenic Hogan was my *grandfather*.

Though I started my Irish tour in County Kerry and found it an incomparable experience, I looked toward the visit to Tipperary, Clare, and Limerick, the home of the Hogans, with the keenest anticipation.

I crossed the Shannon on the ferry from Kerry to Clare and headed for Ennis, the largest town in the county. An American whom I met en route named McDonough had invested millions in Dromoland Castle, near Ballyneety. Ballyneety is a well-known name in hunting circles in the United Kingdom and America. The famous Ballyneety Hunt is an annual affair. (It was also the home of a gigantic horse named Snowman, who took me on the wildest ride of my life. All I did was concentrate on staying aboard—Snowman did all the rest. Hours after scaring me half to death, Snowman was used as a training horse for young children.)

Mr. McDonough, who turned out to be a marvelous fellow, suggested golf at Lahinch, a superb golf course; riding at Ballyneety; fishing outside Scariff; the medieval dinner at Knappogue Castle; and an after-dinner drink at the most famous pub in Ireland, Durty Nellies. (That is not a typographical error.)

I took all his recommendations and gained a thrill that will last me a lifetime and that provided the title and theme of this book. It happened at Knappogue Castle, during the medieval dinner, which is a nightly feature there. Only eighty guests can be accommodated in the castle (on this site since the mid-fifteenth century). Unlike Dromoland, which is much newer, manicured and surrounded by a golf course *within* the castle walls, Knappogue is gaunt and stark. It dominates an ancient road network and surveys the battlefields surrounding.

Upon entering, I was greeted by a damsel in medieval costume. She gave me a dazzling smile and a goblet. This drink (honey, lemon, laced with firey liquor) was the "cup of welcome" in ancient days.

There were other beautiful serving damsels in the room, twelve in all, who became part of the chorus that performed during the medieval dinner, which was authentic in all respects. A handsome minstrel opened the pageant with a stirring speech about the two-thousand-year history of Ireland. His accent was pure Dublin, a place where (even the British believe) the best English in the world is spoken. He described the pageant as chronological—and so it was.

The minstrel and chorus told, century by century, the bitter, tragic, glorious history of this small island, of its settlement by the Milesians and Celts and its invasion and savaging by the Vikings, Normans, and English. Absorbing these invaders, or throwing them out, after centuries of anguish, starvation, torture, and death, was a heroic accomplishment.

The pageant was startlingly interrupted and suspended in time for me by the minstrel when he said, "In the year 1690, the English again invaded, so Sarsfield sends a message to a fearless Rapparee, the Galloping Hogan." I damned near choked on my wine, but regained my composure in time to hear the entire ensemble sing:

> *Old Limerick is in danger,*
> *And Ireland is not free;*
> *So Sarsfield sends a message*
> *To a fearless Rapparee—*
> *"Come ride across the Shannon*
> *At the sounding of the drum—*
> *And we'll blow the enemy seige train*
> *To the land of Kingdom Come."*

CHORUS

> *Galloping Hogan, Galloping Hogan,*
> *Galloping all along,*
> *In his saddle is a sabre,*
> *On his lips there is a song;*
> *He's off across the Shannon*
> *To destroy the enemy cannon;*
> *And he goes galloping, he goes galloping,*
> *Galloping, galloping on . . .*

The Rapparee is bearded,
There's a twinkle in his eye;
As he rides into the city,
The Limerick ladies cry:
"Mr. Outlaw, Mr. Outlaw,
Will you tarry here with me?"
"Och! I'm off to Ballyneety,
To blow up a battery!"

So tonight along the Shannon,
By the pale light of the moon,
There flows an eerie brightness,
As of an Indian noon;
Then clippody-clop resounding
Through the lattice of the shade,
The ghost of Galloping Hogan
Goes a-riding down the glade.

Well! I seized the minstrel after dinner, pinned him to the bar at the nearest pub, and badgered him until he wrote out the lyrics for me. I also wrested from him the first good description I'd heard of *rapparee.* The word itself refers to a short staff of very hard wood that the native Irish carried (often hidden in their cloaks) when weapons were denied them by law. It was called a *rapper,* and many an English skull felt its caress.

When the Irish clans were driven off their lands, many of them took to the hills or, more accurately, to the low, rugged mountains which are a feature of much of Ireland. At first, their only weapons were these rappers, hence the name rapparees, by which they were soon known. To the English, it signified outlaw; to the Irish, it meant hope.

As I walked that night before retiring, a brief wave of emotion, thoughts of Sarah Jane Hogan, my mother, and Domenic Hogan, my Fenian grandfather, engulfed me. The Galloping Hogan—"bearded, with a twinkle in his eye"—was coming out of the shadows. The concept for the book was inherent in the name which ascended from my subconscious, *The Quest for the Galloping Hogan!* I would try to tell the story of the spirit and character of the Irish by discovering the life and death of my legendary ancestor. For only in the spirit of the Irish could the long-term solution to the problems in the north be found.

After that marvelous surprise at Knappogue, I couldn't wait to get to

Ardcrony in Tipperary and to Scariff in Clare, from whence the Hogans came.

After seeing another dawn, this time overlooking Lough Derg fed by the River Shannon, I drove to Scariff. The farmers were already out, the carts with the three large milk cans were jaunting along, each driven by an old Irishman, reins in one hand, the other alternately waving to any passing cars and holding an ancient pipe.

I drove slowly up the hill before Scariff, across a bridge over a small stream and into the modest-sized town. I smiled to myself at the sign Turf Accountant on the left side of the street. That's what bookies are called in Ireland. Unbeknownst to me then, the turf accountant was my cousin Matty.

Now famished, I pulled up before a quaint-looking little inn, seeking one of those unbelievable Irish breakfasts. I wasn't disappointed. The waitress was a beautiful young girl, undoubtedly related to the owner.

When she came in with my check, I asked if any of the Hogans or Guilfoyles were about.

"I'm Sarah Hogan's son," I said.

"Sure enough," she said, "John's in the drapery shop right this instant."

I walked less than twenty yards, entered a drapery shop, small only on the street front. It was surprisingly large inside. It had to be—the place was jammed with fabric, every inch except the salescounter and tiny path through the mountains of bolts of cloth.

A handsome, sweet-faced woman was waiting on a lady. Behind her to her left was a tall, gaunt man with deep-set eyes; he looked at me, pointed his finger, and before I could speak, said, with a ghost of a smile, "Culligan."

I said, "Yes."

"You must be Matthew Joseph, but, by God, you're the spitting image of Ernest." Ernest was my older brother, now dead, who had visited Scariff years before me.

We shook hands. His wife, my first cousin, daughter of my Aunt Rose, the sister who stayed in Ireland, held out her hand. "Glory be," she said, "you're Sarah's son, no doubt of that."

From that point on, I entered an abstract and physical world I'd never known. John Guilfoyle said, "Kate will die of joy. She's got your picture with John Kennedy's on her altar. She lights a candle for the poor lad every day. Come!"

I noticed for the first time that John Guilfoyle limped badly. I noted how roughly dressed he was, work shoes, work clothes. He looked at this moment what he was—a farmer. We crossed the main street of Scariff and entered the small "supermarket." Kate O'Beirne, another of Rose's daughters, owned the shop with her husband.

The words were soft and modestly delivered, but the eyes were moist and wonderfully warm. "Mother of God, Aunt Sarah's boy!"

From there to the turf accountant, where the first bottle of the day appeared. It was Jaimeson's Irish. I took my first drink at 10:30 A.M. and don't remember the place, time, or circumstances of my last. The only place we didn't drink was at the police station, where we visited a second cousin, the assistant police chief.

There was a "paper board" company in Scariff, supervised by (who else) another cousin whose cottage was perched on a hill overlooking the factory and most of Scariff. He was a Dublin-educated lawyer.

Our final daylight stop was at the house in which my mother was born. As we approached on foot, John Guilfoyle said, "The old kitchen is still there. Rose built the new place around it."

A sad, beautiful spirit hung over the place for me. The kitchen was very old and quite large. "It had to be," said John, "with himself, your grandmother, eleven girls, and two boys."

We went outside. On the kitchen side, the ground sloped down to the river. I could imagine the sights and sounds at the riverbank when all the Hogan children played and roughhoused there.

John Guilfoyle mellowed with each passing hour. We seemed to have settled down to about one drink per quarter hour when John disappeared briefly into his flatbed truck with apologies. Back he came, shaven and redressed in a good-looking Irish tweed suit. Then I told him about the song I'd heard at Knappogue Castle. He was unsurprised. "Sure, they've been singing that around Clare since 1800."

To the Guilfoyles, the Galloping Hogan was as real as our maternal grandfather Domenic.

The good Irish whiskey loosened our tongues and sharpened our memories. I told John about my mother's last years, when nature mercifully dimmed her eyes and mind to the present. Mother had lived increasingly in the past, talking about Ireland, her girlhood, her father, and the Galloping Hogan.

At this point, John excused himself and came back with a piece of yellowed paper. It bore a brief poem. John said this was our grandfather's favorite poem. I read:

Chiefs and Warriors Tall and Bright;
From Sire to Sire to lead, bequeathed them
In Valor's Morn or Sorrow's Night
To that pure Gem of Nature: freedom.

The paper was parchment, the writing obviously done with a quill pen. It looked centuries old. I experienced a brief chill, thinking that the Galloping Hogan may have held it in his hands.

I found myself repeating the words over and over. Savoring them, then comprehending them. This poem synthesized Brehon Law and the faith of the Irish clans. It bore some of the secret of the indestructibility of the Irish. Ireland had not known freedom for a thousand years, but there was my grandfather, somewhere during the late 1800s, telling his children and grandchildren in the old clan tradition that the pure gem of nature was freedom.

Before him, for hundreds of years, other fathers, grandfathers, bards, and priests had, in the old oral tradition, breathed into each new generation the spirit of the Irish prototype—a Free Man.

John told me what he remembered hearing as a child about the ancient Hogans. There were, he remembered, five Hogan brothers and cousins who held ring forts and later castles in the Hogan territory along the Shannon known as Ardcrony. After Henry VIII broke with Rome, the Hogans, and all the old families, were defeated in battles and their survivors driven off their lands.

The Hogans did not have an easy time of life through the eighteenth, nineteenth, and twentieth centuries, being related to the Galloping Hogan and always under suspicion (rightly, in some cases) of being Fenians.

I mentioned one episode my mother had discussed, the bayoneting of two young Hogans by the Bloody Black and Tans. A shadow crossed the now relaxed face of John Guilfoyle.

"Aye," he said, "they were little more than babies. They were caught at the bridge at Innisfall by the blackguards and hacked to pieces."

When I left for Kilkenny, Limerick, and then Shannon airport for my return to America, John, Kate, and other assorted Guilfoyles and O'Beirnes stood outside the house where the Hogan girls were born, waving good-bye. I knew I'd be back—and the next time for long enough to find the Galloping Hogan and, with him, the spirit of the Irish and, perhaps, an answer to the terrible problems in Northern Ireland.

2 🍀 My Marvelous French Ally in America

AT THIS juncture in production of the book and shortly after my return to New York, fate (or the luck of the Irish) took a firm hand.

A lady of brief acquaintance named Virginia Dixon asked me to meet Baron Pierre de Neufville. "A real baron?" I asked. Virginia assured me *this* baron was real indeed. She told me little more than that he was an investment banker with Lehman Brothers, wanted to become a merchandising personality, and had an idea for a book. My reaction: "Oh Lord, here we go again." One of my weaknesses has been overaccessibility to anyone with an idea.

But I agreed to meet him. It was arranged, and I was the last to enter a room in which I literally could feel good—or was it mischievously expectant—energy. The reason was immediately apparent. The five other people, with barely suppressed mirth, were laying in wait to see my reaction to the Baron Pierre Phillipe de Neufville, whose right eye bears a black patch, as does my left.

The baron proved a most delightful gentleman. He obviously disliked talking about himself, but he knew we all questioned his credentials. He had an excerpt from the French *armoir*, the almanac of Norman French nobility. It described the de Neufvilles in great detail, establishing the eponymous ancestor as having ruled over nine villages (hence the name Neufville) since about the year A.D. 1000.

I agreed to help him with his book, and a relationship started that— even if it hadn't been for his astonishing assistance with my Quest—has matured into a warm friendship.

I told Pierre about my hopes and aspirations regarding the Galloping Hogan, with a casual reference to the family rumor that he had joined the army of Louis XIV in the region dominated by Dunkirk, of later fame in World War II.

Pierre, deeply motivated by his sense of history, volunteered to make inquiries "with my dearest friend, Patrick MacMahon, in Paris." The name was so Irish-sounding that I laughed. Pierre told me that Le Comte Patrick de MacMahon was the great, great, great grandson of Mahon, one of the Wild Geese of Ireland who became a general of Louis XIV.

My excitement mounted with fragmentary reports that the French Army records for that period had not been destroyed, as had so many records in bombings and burnings during the wars from 1700 through 1945. Several Hogans had military records. Most of the citations concerned a lieutenant, then captain, Hogan and were dated from 1691 through 1727. "My God," I reacted, "that's thirty-six years!" I pleaded with Pierre to ask Le Comte de MacMahon to get copies of key documents. One fine day in October of 1976, Pierre called me: "Good news!" His voice seemed to smile. "I got a package from Patrick this morning. Thirteen documents, crammed with data."

I stupidly asked, "in French?"

"But, of course," Pierre said. "These are machine copies of the records from the official archives of the French army."

I rushed a messenger to Lehman Brothers; he galloped back to me with the package. I could make out occasional words and parts of sentences. These conclusions were made from the February 26, 1726 document:

There was a Jean Hogan who was younger than the Galloping Hogan.

There was a Michael Hogan who led a unit of Irish coexiles to France in 1691, which was retained intact.

The garrison of the regiment was at Arras in Normandy (by a wild coincidence the area of the de Neufvilles, my benefactor in this fact-finding enterprise).

The first major battle in which they fought was the Battle of Lusara.

Jean had several relatives, besides his brothers, who were lieutenant colonels in the Regiment of Clare.

The senior Hogan, first initial M, became a lieutenant general in the army of the King of Portugal.

I could neither read nor speak Portuguese. I knew I would be a most inept researcher in Portugal without substantial clues. I telephoned the Portuguese embassy in Washington, planning my words carefully. After getting the chief military aide on the phone, I said, "One of my ancestors joined the Portuguese army in the early 1700s. Could you help me find out what he did and where and how he died?"

"But, of course," was the enthusiastic answer. "Hold on, sir, I have a copy of the Portuguese military *armoir.*"

I waited with increasing excitement. I was totally unprepared for what happened. He said, "Amazing, Mr. Culligan. There are *four* Hogans listed in the military *armoir.*"

"Is there a Michael Hogan?" I asked.

"No," he said, "there is an A. Hogan, two Hogans with the initial J., one Hogan with the initial D."

"Is there a *General* Hogan?" I pleaded.

"Mr. Culligan," he said, slightly astonished, "there are *three* General Hogans, and one adjutant."

"Did they all serve about the same time?"

"Oh, no, *there* is a difference. Let me see. A. Hogan and the two J. Hogans were much older than D. Hogan."

"Ah," I said, "D. Hogan could have been the son of one of the others."

"Give me a moment," the aide said, "I will read what it says about D. Hogan. Mmm, he started as a lieutenant in 1723; he was promoted to captain in 1728." There was a long pause. I could feel the mood change. He said, "You are in for a shock, Mr. Culligan. The last entry in the Portuguese military *armoir* says that D. Hogan was arrested by the Portuguese Inquisition."

"Oh, my God!" I gasped. "What was he charged with?"

The aide said somberly, "For being a member of the Masonic Order."

"A Portuguese Inquisition?" I asked. "We never heard much about that."

"Well, fortunately," the aide said, "it wasn't like the Spanish Inquisition—more like the French. But no Portuguese is very proud of that inquisition, mild as it was."

The aide became cool and reticent. He excused himself with, "There is reference here to a book *Um Inquerido,* by B. Suerto. All I can suggest is that you get someone in Portugal to check it for you. I am certain that there is no copy outside Portugal." He obviously wanted to terminate the conversation. He said, "I'm sorry."

Not half as sorry as I am, I thought. I was struck by the sheer irony of what I had heard. To have survived the battles of Ireland and France and Portugal, only to end up in a dungeon—or worse. If D. Hogan was arrested and imprisoned, would not the other Hogans have shared this fate?

Then my natural optimism surfaced. The Portuguese were unusually civilized, even in those terrible days. There was no evidence that the Portuguese Inquisition was as brutal and bloody as the Spanish Inquisition. And, what choice did I have in any case? Three Hogans were generals, the other adjutant of a major cavalry post. Imprisonment, yes, banishment, perhaps, but I couldn't accept the idea of torture and execution at that point.

My research plan was organized rapidly then. It would be Ireland first, then France with a superb contact, Le Comte Patrick de MacMahon, then Portugal, where the trail might end in disaster. Then, if necessary, the Eternal City, the Vatican in Rome.

3 🍀 My Irish Allies

YOU GET the sense of Ireland in the Celtic Lounge at Kennedy International Airport. The lilting brogue of the hostess works that minor magic. The plane ride to Ireland was uneventful. The sweet-faced, older lady who sat next to me was troubled. She sighed deeply, inadvertently, several times. We spoke when the cocktails arrived. It was a sad mission for her.

"My mother is dying. She might be gone by the time I get there," she said. I encouraged her to talk, which she did, telling me of her emigration to America, her unsuccessful marriage, more than compensated for by two lovely children and four grandchildren. Then she uttered a single sentence that spoke volumes about the role and attitude of many Irish women of her generation who were raised "to bear and forbear." She said, "Well, I guess I did what was expected of me." This without defiance or resignation.

The weather as we neared Ireland was foul and gusty. The plane hit, bounded high into the air, hit again, bounded again, then settled firmly on the runway. There was a long pause, then a well-lubricated, heavily brogued voice rang out, "Great fookin' landin', all three of them." There was appreciative, if embarrassed, laughter.

The ride into Dublin is much more enjoyable if one does what the experienced traveler in Ireland does—ride in the front with the driver. Dublin cab drivers are invariably friendly, and sometimes funny, men. Mine, Michael Mahon, had a ready supply of Dublin chatter and jokes.

I contracted with Michael to drive me around Dublin and the nearby counties. While I was overcoming jet lag, I had him drive me to one place close to Dublin of special magic to me. It is described as the Meeting of the Waters. Three rivers come to confluence in a metaphysical setting, which Thomas Moore described.

> Sweet vale of Avoca! how calm could I rest
> In thy bosom of shade, with the friends I love best,
> Where the storms that we feel in this cold world should cease,
> And our hearts, like thy waters, be mingled in peace.

With the memory of that exquisite sentiment as a palliative, I slept and gathered strength for the Irish dawn. I arrived in downtown Dublin on a day so dreary that it tested the good nature of even the typical Irishman who described almost any rainy day as "a soft day." The first evening was spent at the Edwardian bar of Buswell's Hotel, directly across from the Irish Parliament. It was a good choice, as was my position at the bar. I had less than half my first drink when I was drawn into a group who had a considerable head start with the potent Irish whiskey. Conor Cruise O'Brien had been in the news that day. One of the group was not a fan of the Honorable Conor Cruise O'Brien, who became known around the world during his service to the United Nations.

Another, who obviously didn't want things to get too serious, said, "I met one of his relatives recently, a saxaphonist named Conor Blues O'Brien."

"Oh, it's a large family," said another. "A cousin is a prizefighter, Conor Bruise O'Brien."

"There is a poor relative in Dublin, a chimney sweep," offered another, "Conor Flues O'Brien."

The game got hotter. There were:

the publican	Conor Booze O'Brien
Sherlock Holmes's associate	Conor Clues O'Brien
the practical joker	Conor Ruse O'Brien
the golf-club delinquent	Conor Overdues O'Brien
the incorrigible gambler	Conor Lose O'Brien

not to mention the hermit	Conor Recluse O'Brien
and the labor negotiator	Conor Refuse O'Brien
of course, the well-known lawyer	Conor Sues O'Brien
the parish priest	Conor Pews O'Brien
the investigative reporter	Conor News O'Brien
the black-sheep pool sharp	Conor Cues O'Brien
and my sole contribution, the narcoleptic	Conor Snooze O'Brien

Much, perhaps too much, has been written about Irish pubs and drinking. Both are there in profusion. Most of it is very good-natured socializing, and for the many Irish farmers, laboring in the often damp and chilly fields, the pubs offer a warm and pleasant haven.

My first contact in Dublin was Seamus Kelly, a veteran newsman of the *Irish Times* and a constructive delight. We spoke via telephone first, and he seemed pleased at the prospect of helping. He suggested a favorite Dublin meeting place, a pub named Tobins on Duke Street. He held that I'd recognize him in a green suit and a dark shirt. I rejoined that I'd be wearing a black patch on my left eye, not easy to miss. He laughed, "This will be jolly good. A lady meeting me wears a patch too. You can play snaps."

I got to Tobins first, then came Seamus. He was fascinating looking, white-haired, spade-bearded, slender, of twinkling eye. Then two ladies arrived, slender and handsome in tweeds. One did have a patch on her right eye, held in place by a contraption I couldn't figure out. We never did get around to playing snaps. Seamus Kelly, looking at us, said, "By God, it looks like Raphael Sabbatini wrote the script for this meeting."

After multiple drinks, Seamus asked how he could help, and I told him. He sparked, "Colonel Pat Hogan is a dear friend. He runs the barracks at the Curragh. He's a *Hogan*—do you think you might be related?"

The Curragh is the center of thoroughbred horse activity in Ireland. It literally stretches as far as the eye can see and contains, in one corner, the biggest military base in Ireland.

"Call Pat. Tell him you're a friend of mine."

I did. His warmth and friendliness flowed through the telephone. "I'm here Monday to Friday and in Dublin on weekends. What would suit you?"

I seized the opening and asked if I could come to the barracks at about three the next day. I calculated that my interview would run into tea-time, which in an Irish officer's mess had to be a unique experience. It did, and it was.

All the officers except the duty officer assembled in the sparsely furnished officers' mess. Colonel Pat Hogan introduced me to the group, then named each officer, who acknowledged with a grin and wave of the hand. The orderlies entered with tea, the superb brown soda bread, butter and jams and marmalade. There was good-natured banter among the other officers and obvious deference to the colonel, for sufficient reason. In addition to his thirty-four years of military experience, he had a worldwide reputation as an officer of three UN peace missions— in the Congo, the Near East, and Cyprus. He had distinguished himself and gained kudos for Ireland by competent, objective evenhandedness. After tea, Colonel Hogan and I returned to his office, his interest in my project remaining high.

He was intrigued by the thirteen pages of copies of original records from the Ministère de la Défense, État-Mayor de Larmee de Terre, Service Historique, 94300 Château de Vincennes, du 75947, Paris.

In this friendly atmosphere, I asked about his birthplace. I was elated when he said "Tipperary." That was Hogan land. His physical resemblance to other Hogans of the family was striking, but I pursued the relationship idea no further at that time.

Colonel Hogan was delighted when I offered him copies of these documents. He outdid himself to reciprocate, disclosing a new resource for my study. There was a unit, he said, whose sole purpose was gaining and keeping records on all Irish exiles in the military service of other governments. This would provide an invaluable source for cross-checking with the French and Portuguese military resources.

He opened one other possible avenue: Spain. Many of the Wild Geese went there, and, although I had no evidence that any Hogans went, it was worth checking out. Colonel Hogan described the unit as having thousands of index cards, one for each exile. He then made his final major contribution: he called the lady in charge of the unit and secured her promise that she would identify and trace all the Clare, Tipperary, and Limerick Hogans in the files. Months of work were thus saved by a telephone call and the sweet talk of the gracious Colonel Hogan.

Equally important was his caution regarding Irish family histories.

He advised, "Matthew, one piece of unbiased evidence from *outside* Ireland is worth dozens of self-seeking bits of semifiction from questionable sources. It isn't just the Irish imagination and ego that is responsible, but the fact that the English had control of all communications from Ireland for centuries. It wasn't to their advantage to let the rest of the world know that they were wrecking a country that had an older and, in some ways, better culture than they did."

"That's part of the spoils of war, Pat," I said, "control of the writing and the obliteration and the rewriting of history."

Later that evening, I reworked my research plan. I decided to spend half as much time in Ireland as originally planned and twice as much in France, Portugal, and Rome.

The next morning I called the archivist cited by Pat Hogan as keeper of the records of the Wild Geese, the scores of thousands of Irish who fled Ireland to escape the death, imprisonment, starvation, and degradation imposed upon them by the English. This migration (and, hence, the records) started in 1602. A quiet, beautifully modulated voice invited me to an initial visit because, "I'm not sure I can help."

Her "office" was at the University of Dublin at Earlsfort Terrace, a block off Saint Stephen's Green. I went down two levels, past various thought-provoking departments of the medical school—virology, pathology, forensic medicine—and then I was startled to see, right next to the door marked Archives, the sign

FORBIDDEN—DANGEROUS TO HUMAN LIFE.

I edged past that door and entered the archives quickly.

Micheline Walsh was a tiny, beautiful woman of indeterminable age. I asked her, "My God, what's next door, germ-warfare research?"

She laughed. "No, that's the electric transformer. I suppose it *is* dangerous to human life."

I started the meeting by giving her all the material on the Hogans I had from the French army archives. She was delighted and reciprocated with a promise to search her files for Ógans, O'Hogans, and Hogans. Not just in France but in Spain as well. I told her what Pat Hogan had said about bogus Irish history. "Oh, yes," she agreed, "one really disreputable bit of evidence in a batch can disqualify everything. Try to get some facts from qualified *unfriendly* sources.

"There was a chaplain with the Williamite army—his name was Storey. He wrote some vivid reports about Sarsfield, and several reports about the Rapparees will surprise you. They couldn't have made the Williamite officers very happy."

"Where can I get hold of these?" I asked.

"Alice Curtayne wrote a good book about Sarsfield's life. There is one chapter on Sarsfield's Ride and the Galloping Hogan's part in it." She added, "If you can't find a copy, I'll *lend* you mine." The emphasis on "lend" was with a smile.

"How much information do you have on the Wild Geese in Portugal?" I asked.

"Not much yet," she replied. "Most of the Wild Geese went to France and advanced very well in rank. A lesser, but significant number went to Spain. We know some went to Austria—the Austro-Hungarian Empire that is. And others did go to Portugal. One of the most tragic aspects of the Wild Geese was that they too often fought on *both* sides in some battles."

"You know, Micheline," I said, "that might very well have been the strategy of the English, to get the young Irishmen and officers out of Ireland on almost any basis, knowing that they could do little other than become mercenaries and kill and be killed by Dutchmen, Spaniards, Germans, and Portuguese. Sarsfield, I understand, was killed at the Battle of Landen in Flanders."

"Yes," agreed Micheline Walsh. "And too many Irishmen killed their own countrymen in duels while they were in the same units. We know it got so bad that King Louis XIV outlawed dueling in the French army. In fact, while you were on your way over I checked the files. A General Hogan was court-martialed for killing an Irish officer named Conway in a duel. Here is the report in French, as it is recorded in the French army archives. I added the English translation."

The report read:

Bibliothèque Nationale, Paris.
Département des Manuscrits.
Chérin 59, Folio 7.

Jacques Conway, écuyer, second fils, Capitaine dans le Régiment de Montcashell infanterie au service de France, fut tué dans un duel en France par le Général Hogan. Il épousa 1° la soeur du Général Pierse de qui il n'eut point d'enfant, 2° Mademoiselle O Driscol de qui il eut deux fils tous deux officiers au service d'Espagne.

(James Conway, esquire, second son, Captain in the Regiment of Mountcashel, infantry, in the service of France, was killed in a duel in France by General Hogan. He married: 1, the sister of General Pierse by whom he had no children; 2, Mademoiselle O Driscol by whom he had two sons both of whom became officers in the service of Spain.)

Micheline gave me that information so fast and casually that I didn't at first realize its import. If General Hogan fought an illegal duel, that could be the reason for his switching armies, from France to Portugal.

"No first name in that report," I said.

"No, but there was only one General Hogan in the French army, many colonels, and captains, only one general."

"The same Michael Hogan," I replied.

I commented on the quality of the French military records, and she extolled their excellence, but said many were destroyed in World War One and World War Two. She showed me the following sample of how the French traced Irish officers' genealogies.

			Christopher Conway of Dromulton, Co.	=	Joanna Roche		
			Kerry raised a company of volunteers for				
			the service of James I [sic]. Killed at				
			Aughrim in 1691.				

Edmund	James	Thomas	Joseph of	Jenkin d.s.p.	Robert	Christopher	Elisabeth
lieutenant in	captain in	volunteer in	Conway		d.s.p.	married	married
his father's	Mountcashel's	the army of	House, Co.			Catherine	Deniss
company.	regiment	James II.	Clare.			Hussey.	O'Connell of
Killed at	in France.	Married					Derrinane,
Aughrim	Killed by	Anne					Co. Kerry.
1691 d.s.p.	General	Fitzgerald.					[This is the
Was married	Hogan.						O'Connel
to Joanna	Married: 1,						clan from
Fitzgerald of	sister of						which
Ardglass.	General						Daniel
	Pierse, 2,						O'Connel
	Mlle.						sprang.]
	O'Driscol.						

From information preserved in: Bibliothèque Nationale, Paris, Département des Manuscrits; Chérin 59

Then, with a warm smile, Micheline Walsh handed me two more documents, English translations of records of Hogans marked *Bibliothèque Nationale, Paris, Pièces Originales.*

The first read:

Wee the undernamed doe herebye certifie that Capt. John Hogan is a Gentleman borne being the son of Bryan O'Hogan gentleman, the grandson of Thomas O'Hogan of Ardcrony Esq. being originally descended of an ancient and noble family in Lower Ormond, beinge commonly known Ardcrony where the sd. family was possest of considerable estates of inheritance and matched into the nobility and Gentry of ye sd. Kingdom of Ireland, always known Roman Catholicks and Loyall to ye Crown. Dated at Paris this [sic] day July 1700.

C. Callaghan   Cha. Macartie   Oliver Grace

The second stated:

Wee the undernamed doe certifie and attest that Patrick Hogan, gentle-man, is the son of Morgan Hogan, gentleman, the son of Richard Hogan, gentleman, son of Ogan O'Hogan Chiefe of the familie of the O'Hogans in the County of Tipperary and of Margaret Conway daughter of Thomas Conway of Glanduff in the County of Lymerick, and that the said families enjoyed considerable ancient estates of inheritance in the said counties of Tipperary and Lymerick in the Kingdom of Ireland.
Dated at St. Germain the 12th of March, 1699

Bryttas

Micheline and I parted with mutual promises to meet again soon.

With my decision to spend less time in Ireland and more looking back through the eyes of the French and Portuguese, I spent my time in Ireland concentrating on the last half of the seventeenth century.

Despite the good progress in research, one nagging worry remained. What would be the central focus of the book? One of the editors who did express interest asked, "Possibly of considerable interest to Irish-Americans, what about the rest of us?"

Another said, "Apparently, quite a family—the Hogans. Did they all become mercenaries . . . ?"

There was a clue in the opinion of the editor I respected the most. "Could *The Quest for the Galloping Hogan* cast some light on the horrible mess in the North?"

I said, "I hope so."

Awareness of the complexity of the native Irish was coming in on me through all the senses. The native Irish were very different from the Irish in America. The native Irish *needed* heroes. They were emerging almost like sleepwalkers from the shock of being free and independent. John F. Kennedy was such a hero; his death hit the Irish more than it hit most Americans. The Galloping Hogan was a legendary hero from the last romantic period in Irish history. If he left Ireland with the Wild

Geese in 1691, I would have the opportunity to tell the story of this gallant band of exiles.

Three of the leaders of the Wild Geese who left Ireland in 1691 were Michael Hogan, who commanded an Irish unit kept intact by the French; Patrick Sarsfield, who also became a general; and Mahon, who did the same. Sarsfield and Mahon later became marshals of France, and Mahon married a French noblewoman and started the MacMahon line of France.

Other Irishmen of note among the important of other countries were: Count Taffee, descendant of a Roscommon family, premier of Austria-Hungary in both 1868 and 1893; a prime minister of Spain, Leopold O'Donnell, a descendant of the great Hugh O'Donnell; and Leopold O'Donnell's son, Charles, prime minister of Spain in the twentieth century.

Aristide Briand, of Irish ancestry, was eleven times premier of France. He was the great-great-grandson of Conal O'Brien, of the Dalcassian chieftains. A president of Mexico, General Alvaro Obregon was a descendant of a member of the Wild Geese.

Observers thought it strange that a lady named Josephine de Gaulle wrote a biography of Daniel O'Connell and that Charles de Gaulle was pleased to vacation in Ireland. It became understandable when it was learned that his great-grandfather married Josephine MacCarten, an Irish lady.

The Galloping Hogan would not have had even the tiniest footnote in Irish history, however, were it not for Patrick Sarsfield, Earl of Lucan. He was the beacon that illuminated the Galloping Hogan.

Where I would end up in my quest could not even be guessed. But my starting point had to be Patrick Sarsfield, who called for the Galloping Hogan and rode with him to immortality.

4 🍀 The Ireland of Patrick Sarsfield and the Galloping Hogan

Cromwell in Ireland, disposing of overwhelming strength and using it with merciless wickedness, debased the standards of human conduct and sensibly darkened the journey of mankind.

WINSTON CHURCHILL,
A History of the English-Speaking Peoples

IN SOME respects, the blackest year in the whole history of the British Isles was 1649. On January 30 of that year, King Charles I was beheaded, and the English Commonwealth was established. In 1653, Oliver Cromwell became known as the Protector.

The monarchy had lost, the parliamentary army had won, but the army itself then became a threat. The army had to be disbursed, or at least divided. Tragically for Ireland, and also for England, the monstrous Oliver Cromwell used the law of retribution against Catholic Ireland as an expeditious duality: it satisfied the hatred of the extreme reformationists, the militant Protestants against the Catholics, and it got much of the army out of England.

First, the holy war against the Irish Catholics was used to screen out soldiers who would not fight in that war. Only the most rabid Protestant soldiers and officers were retained in the invading army. Cromwell joined with the Puritan Divines in creating a holy war upon the Irish. It was essential, in the evil mind of Cromwell, partly as a lesson to England to prevent a ferocious social revolution there.

Cromwell's campaign was among the most carefully calculated and merciless in all modern history. He decreed a campaign of "designed frightfulness" that would spread a "useful terror" throughout Ireland and give a mirror image to the English, who were seeking, among other things, land reform.

No better testament is possible than this report to John Bradshaw, President of the English Council of State:

> It has pleased God to bless our endeavors at Drogheda. After battery, we stormed it. The enemy were about three thousand strong in the town. They made a stout resistance. . . . Being thus entered, we refused them quarter, having the day before summoned the town. I believe we put to the sword the whole number of defendants. . . . This has been a marvelous great mercy. The enemy, not willing to put an issue upon a field battle, had put into this garrison almost all their prime soldiers, under command of their best officers. I do not believe that any officer escaped with his life . . . the enemy upon this were filled with much terror. And truly I believe this bitterness will save much effusion of blood, through the goodness of God.
>
> I wish that all honest hearts may give the glory of this to God alone, to Whom indeed the praise of this mercy belongs.

The author of this report: *Oliver Cromwell.*

In another letter to a member of parliament, Cromwell exulted that he had heard one Irish casualty, trapped in a burning church, which Cromwell ordered set aflame, scream "I burn, I burn!" Cromwell wrote, in part, "I am persuaded that this is a righteous judgment of God upon these barbarous wretches."

Winston Churchill, whose father Randolph did great damage to Ireland by whipping up the Scottish-English Protestants in Ireland against the native Catholic Irish in the north, perhaps best described the long-term results of Cromwell's God-politics frightfulness:

> Cromwell in Ireland, disposing of overwhelming strength, and using it with merciless wickedness, debased the standards of human conduct and sensibly darkened the journey of mankind. Cromwell's Irish massacres find numberless compeers in the history of all countries during and since the Stone Age. . . . By an uncompleted process of terror, by an iniquitous land settlement, by the virtual proscription of the Catholic religion, by the bloody deeds already described, he cut new gulfs between the nations and the creeds. . . . Upon us all there still lies "the curse of Cromwell."

The implication is naked: the frightfulness of Cromwell's holy war against the Catholics of Ireland poisoned almost all Irishmen to some degree, and some Irishmen fatally.

He also had a special black place in the hearts of other of his countrymen than Winston Churchill. His own personal physician had this to say of his deceased patient. Cromwell was "a perfect master of all the arts of simulation and of dissimulation; who turning up the whites of his eyes, and seeking the Lord with pious gestures, would weep and pray and cant most devoutly till the opportunity offered to deal his dupe a knock-down blow under the short ribs."

Cromwell's holy war set the stage for the counterattacks of the Irish, who nursed their terrible wounds until later generations, then resumed the rebellion against England. The ultimate insult of one Irishman to another was, "The curse of Cromwell upon ye."

The "luck of the Irish" is a recent phenomenon. They were tragically unlucky in 1649, when Cromwell used the Irish holy war to break up the parliamentary army which had deposed Charles I and effected his beheading. The Irish were fated to ill luck once again when James II, the only Catholic English king since the Reformation, outraged the Protestants and led them to invite William of Orange to invade England on behalf of Protestantism.

William of Orange landed in England in 1688. The army of King James faded away, and he went into exile in France instead of to the execution block. The reward of William of Orange was another war against the Irish, where James landed in 1689 with the hope of using his base in Ireland as a stepping-stone to win back the English crown.

William's well-equipped army was invincible, and more Scottish and English settlers poured into Ireland, seizing the best land from the routed Irish. Thus 1689 helped set the stage for the drama being played out to this day in Londonderry and its capital city, Belfast.

That was the situation in Ireland during the closing years of the seventeenth century: the bloody frightfulness of Cromwell, the disenfranchisement of the native Irish Catholics in Ulster, and the threat of a similar disenfranchisement in the south as the victorious English army turned south toward Clare, Tipperary, Kerry, Cork, Sligo, Mayo, and Limerick.

The situation seemed hopeless. The English army had field artillery in quantity and gunners who knew how to use it, hot from the Battle of the Boyne, which had settled the fate of the native Irish in the north. But two major developments occurred which saved southern Ireland.

A glamorous, able, and fearless leader, Patrick Sarsfield, rose and inspired the remnants of the Irish forces in a spirited defense of the city of Limerick. He understood the deep interest of King Louis XIV of France in keeping the English army of William of Orange pinned down in Ireland while Louis's armies overran Belgium. England had guaranteed the protection of Belgium, and King William could not run the risk of his total loss of credibility.

William wanted to end the English involvement in Ireland quickly and totally, in order to send the promised aid to Belgium. His best hope lay with the huge siege train of artillery, men, and horses that was approaching Limerick, with which he would, he hoped, destroy the city and with it southern Ireland's defense.

Patrick Sarsfield called for the Galloping Hogan, who had been outlawed by the English and had a price on his head, to lead him on the famous ride to Ballyneety where they met and destroyed this siege train. This was the Galloping Hogan who became immortalized in the song that has been sung in County Clare since 1800.

By all accounts, the Galloping Hogan was a fiercely independent Rapparee. That he would answer the call of Sarsfield speaks well for Sarsfield's leadership qualities and charisma. Fortunately for me, Sarsfield, as the Earl of Lucan, had considerable historical visibility around the county and city of Limerick.

These are the facts, legends, and speculations:

There were five bands of Rapparees operating very effectively in Ireland during the battles between King James and King William.

Patrick Sarsfield reported that he was surrounded by associates who had sent word to King William that they would desert King James and the Irish cause (they did).

The number of people Patrick Sarsfield could trust was limited to his closest military aides—and one other, the Galloping Hogan.

Patrick Sarsfield rode out of Limerick in the black of night with key officers and 500 picked troopers, whom he placed entirely in the hands of the Galloping Hogan. He trusted the Galloping Hogan and this trust propelled Patrick Sarsfield into historical immortality.

Patrick Sarsfield's ancestry was Norman, Gallo-Celtic, evident in his name, Patrick (distinctly Norman), his coloring (reddish blond), and his size (he was described as "huge"). Patrick's mother was Ann O'Moore, daughter of the legendary "Rory of the Hills," who led the

Uprising of 1641, which in turn fanned the flames of the horror of Cromwell. It is important in this context, because the first ten years of Patrick's life were spent in the designed frightfulness of Cromwell's religious war.

There were over nine generations of intermarriage for the Sarsfields in Ireland, a heady mixture that reached back into the mists of antiquity. The ultimate blend was middle European, German, Milesian, Celtic, Norman, and Danish.

This meager bit is known about Patrick Sarsfield between his birth and 1690. He was smuggled out of Ireland at about age twelve to France for his early Catholic education. He was then enrolled in a French military academy for preparation as a soldier and statesman, at least as far as languages and European politics were concerned. He spoke French, Gaelic, and English. His older brother had married a sister of the Duke of Monmouth. Through this connection, he won a commission as an ensign in the duke's regiment.

He had good fortune in being exposed to the Duke of Luxembourg, the greatest living military strategist of the age. He was Louis XIV's foremost general. The present country bearing his name was given to Luxembourg as a reward for his services to Louis. The young Sarsfield rose dramatically in the regiment of the Duke of Monmouth, from ensign to lieutenant to captain in less than eight years. The scent of a plot surrounds his next move to England to join the army of Charles II, a very unlikely event unless, as was rumored (and later confirmed), Charles had secretly become a Catholic.

Sarsfield fought in battles and in at least one duel as a second. During those days the seconds fought along with their principals. Sarsfield received wounds, the first of many, which brought him near death. The next was a wound suffered when he repulsed an attack against the royal army by Monmouth. A farmer warned Sarsfield about the imminent surprise night attack, and Sarsfield was prepared and routed his attackers, but he fell and was left for dead on the battlefield.

He vaulted to fame when he recovered and his exploits were reported to James II, then king of England. In the mode of the time, he was given a grant of land in County Kildare. Around 1690, Sarsfield married one of the most famous beauties of Ireland, Honoré, the daughter of the Earl of Clanricarde.

All was well with Patrick at this juncture. His brother had died without an heir. Patrick became the Earl of Lucan, adding the Lucan estates to those he owned in Kildare. His courage, stature, ancestry, and military training made him the logical leader of the Irish at Limerick, confused and concerned as they were by the dreadful news of the English victory at the Boyne and the horror stories of the English artillery.

The English army raced in close pursuit of the remnants of the Irish army, followed by the siege train with five hundred horses, baggage, and dozens of cannons which would, the commanders thought, level the walls of Limerick in short order. The rest would be no less than the downfall of Catholic Ireland.

The instructions of William of Orange were to end the Irish war with all possible haste. There were agonized pleas from the Belgian allies, who saw the French invasion being prepared. The fates of Patrick Sarsfield and the Galloping Hogan became entwined.

5 🍀 The Galloping Hogan

'Tis Ireland hath need of him,
And him alone to-day!

PERCY FRENCH,
" 'Galloping' O'Hogan"

SINCE THERE were no public historical records about the Galloping Hogan before his identification as a friend and ally of Patrick Sarsfield, I determined to find out if any church records existed. The Roman Catholic clergy went underground after the Cromwell victory. But surviving underground was no new challenge to the Catholic priests and their more devout followers, and so it was through a priest I met in Dublin that I was introduced to a priest who was head of a small monastery in the Dalcassian territory.

The Dublin priest was Father Henry, a member of the Capuchin Order. He was editor of the *Capuchin Annual*, a superb publication for historians, scholars, and patriotic Irish men and women.

Our meeting was almost accidental. I was actually on the trail of another ancestor, John Hogan, a sculptor who lived between 1800 and 1856. The *Capuchin Annual* had devoted a dozen or so loving pages to him, calling him the greatest sculptor of his time. It was in this context that I met Father Henry. When I told him that my interest extended beyond John Hogan to the Galloping Hogan, he grinned delightedly and volunteered his help.

I asked him for help in two ways: I needed to know how the clans lived while the Galloping Hogan was growing up; and I needed to know the first name of the Galloping Hogan.

Father Henry told me of the monastery which, he said, had several large rooms crammed with the written reports of priests and Jesuits, from the fifteenth to the seventeenth centuries. So the next morning I drove to the monastery and introduced myself to the abbot as a friend of Father Henry. His greeting was so warm, I knew Father Henry had called him. This was speedily confirmed when he brought out his rare copy of the *Capuchin Annual,* the issue bearing the article by C. P. Curren on John Hogan.

I realized then that my sly friend, Father Henry, had told the monastery head about my interest in John Hogan the sculptor, but not about my passion for the old manuscripts. I reasoned that Father Henry was afraid I would not be entirely welcome as a complete stranger. My host took such delight in giving me what he had on John Hogan that I quickly became convinced Father Henry had played the scene exactly right. My host shared the view of Father Henry that John Hogan was the best sculptor in Ireland, England, and Scotland during his time, and probably the best in Europe and the Mediterranean as well. My host identified with John Hogan far more than I did at the moment. He gave me this brief poem written as a tribute to John Hogan:

> *Battling through years, with many a haunting care*
> *He scaled the shadowy golden heights,*
> *Gave Rome the sculptor's share.*

"From all accounts, John Hogan was a simple and delightful artist who didn't take himself too seriously," my host said. "This is an excerpt from a letter John Hogan wrote in November 1828."

> I hope in God, Father Mac Namara may succeed in his kind intentions toward me, as it is on his exertions that my present fate depends, if he could . . . enable me to purchase a fine block of marble and pay for the embossing. I should be content to live on macaroni and sugar until such times as it would be finished. It is said that this work of mine, *The Dead Christ* . . . ranks me as a sculptor.

That work, *The Dead Christ*, did indeed raise John Hogan to the first rank of sculptors in Rome. As a result of it he was made a member of the Virtuosi of the Parthenon, the only sculptor in Ireland, England,

and Scotland to be so honored by his peers. I looked at the picture of *The Dead Christ* and found it profoundly moving. I said so.

"You are not alone, Mr. Culligan," my host said. "Some very cynical critics said it was one of the finest works of its time. There was a very successful newspaper in those days, *The Limerick Reporter*, it was called. This is what the art critic of that newspaper said of *The Dead Christ.*"

> *Oh wondrous marble . . . here we see*
> *really portrayed in thee*
> *that reed, the thorns, the nails, behold*
> *the tale too well too truly told.*
> *Ah . . . who could turn unmoved, away*
> *from all those bitter emblems say?*
> *But pause, and weep, and weeping feel*
> *'tis no idolatory to kneel.*

We were almost reverently silent for a moment. Then I commented on the early death of John Hogan, at fifty-six years of age.

"Well, he died of a broken heart, it is said," responded my host.

"Really, you mean with that much talent, he was . . ." I didn't finish.

My host said, "You will find, Mr. Culligan, if you haven't already found, there is a dark side to the Irish personality. It was labeled 'the accursed vice of the Irish' by an Italian Papal Nuncio, who was sent to Ireland in the seventeenth century by the Pope. Mind you, this Cardinal loved Ireland and had many wonderful things to say about the Irish, but he wrote in a report that 'the spirit of rivalry and jealousy is the accursed vice of the Irish.' He went on to say that the Irish paid a terrible price for this spirit of rivalry and jealousy when the invaders came, the Vikings, the Normans, and the Tudor English.

"When John Hogan returned to Ireland in what should have been triumph, he found he had been preceded by rumors that he was forced to leave Rome because he had been sympathetic to some revolutionary movement there."

"Incredible," I said.

"Not only that," continued my host, "John Hogan married a beautiful Italian lady named Speranza. *That*, believe it or not, was resented by some of Ireland's leading ladies."

I felt my moment of truth was coming close. My host made it relatively easy when he asked, proudly, "Would you believe, Mr. Culligan, that a thousand years of history could be compressed into a thirty-line poem?"

I looked very skeptical, to give this charming priest his fun. He said, "The last great moment of glory for John Hogan, in his political sculpture, was the heroic statue of Daniel O'Connell. After he got the commission, while he was envisioning the work, Thomas Davis, a great scholar who was known as Ireland's Teacher, publicly gave this admonition to John Hogan."

> *Let centuries of wrong*
> *Upon his recollections throng*
> *Strongbow's force, and Henry's wile*
> *Tudor's wrath and Stuart's guile*
> *And Iron Stafford's tiger jaws*
> *And Brutal Brunswick's penal laws*
> *Not forgetting Saxon faith*
> *Not forgetting Norman scath*
> *Not forgetting William's word*
> *Not forgetting Cromwell's sword*
> *Let the Union's fether vile*
> *The shame and ruin of our isle*
> *Let trampled altar, rifled urn*
> *Knit his look to purpose stern*
> *Mould all this into one thought*
> *Like wizard cloud with thunder fraught*
> *Still let our glories through it gleam*
> *Like fair flowers through flooded stream*
> *Or like a flashing wave at night*
> *Bright, mid the solemn darkness bright*
> *Let the memory of old days*
> *Shine through statesman's anxious face*
> *Death's power and Brian's fame*
> *And headlong Sarsfield's sword of flame*
> *And the Spirit of Red Hugh*
> *And the pride of eighty-two*
> *And the victories he won*
> *And the hope that leads him on*
> *Chisel thus and thus alone*
> *If to man you'd change the stone.*

I reacted with sincere admiration, then asked, "What was the end like for John Hogan?"

"The end was brought on by his most severe disappointment, the loss of the commission to sculpt the heroic statue of Patrick Sarsfield which the men of Limerick had decided upon as a prominent memorial in that city, which he had defended and saved from destruction."

"He was denied it?" I asked.

"Yes, despite the part played in the ride to Ballyneety by his clansman, the Galloping Hogan, John Hogan was denied that work on which he had set his heart. He had a stroke soon thereafter."

"A sad end, indeed, for a great artist," I mourned.

"One story told by eyewitnesses would indicate that he died in relative peace," my host replied. After he suffered the stroke and could sculpt no more, he felt blessed that his son, John Valentine Hogan, was advanced enough in his own career to complete the unfinished work of his father. Nonetheless, those close to him said he often appeared deeply depressed. Then one day he requested that he be taken to the Church where his *Dead Christ* was permanently displayed. He was observed kneeling before this sculpture. He appeared to be sobbing, but when he rose, his demeanor was markedly changed. He seemed to be at peace. He died not long after, in 1856."

We were reverentially silent for a long moment. Then I judged that the time was right for the disclosure of my mission, the ancient documents.

Instantly this friendly, outgoing Irishman came under obvious stress. He gave me no encouragement initially. Instead he diverted me with a history of the monastery. Then I realized it was no diversion. The monastery was under the supervision of trustees, some laymen, several lawyers. My host was not educated as a lawyer, he advised, so when he was appointed head of the monastery, he was given a lengthy indoctrination about the responsibility of the trustees. It was a multilevel responsibility, encompassing:

The names of the individuals and, in some cases, whole families who renounced their Roman Catholic religion to save their lives and/or their lands. Some of the proudest names in Ireland were involved. They had resumed their Catholicism when it was again safe to do so. This information was a timebomb that no one wanted to set off.

The names of Irish men and some women who informed on fellow clansmen and neighbors to win the favor of the Cromwellians.

The names of some Rapparees who had revenged themselves and their country on Cromwellian soldiers and colonists by "accidents," mainly along the roads and in the forests and bogs.

The locations of hoards of church documents and possessions buried by the priests before they fled or were captured.

The names of scores of priests who were captured and killed by Cromwell's soldiers and colonists. Many were dragged by the feet behind galloping horses. The Jesuits were hanged, drawn, and quartered.

"So, Mr. Culligan," he said, "I am specifically forbidden to give these documents, or copies of them, to anyone."

"Do any of them relate just to how the clans lived before they were driven off their lands?" I asked.

"Oh, yes," he said. "Information of that kind was gathered for the bishops in Ireland and the Vatican."

"A kind of State of the Church," I suggested.

"Exactly," the priest replied. "You know, the Roman Catholic Church may be the oldest continuous administrative force in the world."

"May I ask you this, then," I pleaded. "I am not interested in anything other than how my clansmen lived before being killed in battle with Cromwell's forces or before being driven off their lands. If I promise not to mention the source and use only the description of how the people lived, how their children were taught, would you let me look at only those documents?"

"Would you let me see your notes, when you finish, Mr. Culligan?"

"Of course," I pledged. "That, plus my solemn oath that neither you nor the monastery, nor even the location would ever be disclosed. I'll simply say it was a monastery in what was known as the Dalcassian territory, what is now Clare, Limerick, and Tipperary."

"I'll think about that overnight, Mr. Culligan," he promised. "One more thing. Our documents are priceless and irreplaceable. Also, the property rights laws apply. You may or may not know, Mr. Culligan, that all our documents which are signed by individuals are the property of *their* estates. This monastery, curiously enough, could sell these documents, but could not *publish* them without the permission of the controllers of the estates. I tell you this in case I have to say no tomorrow."

I left, and had a nervous night. Without some authentic facts about clan life, my presentation of the Galloping Hogan would be badly out of balance with that of Patrick Sarsfield.

I called at the monastery the next morning, to be elated immediately by the sight of the abbot's face as he entered the room. He didn't look like a man about to say no.

After a handshake, he said, "I didn't ask any of the trustees. I was afraid they'd say no. I did call Father Henry. He urged me to cooperate under the conditions we described yesterday."

"Thank you from the bottom of my heart, Father," I said. "I'll protect the confidence."

"I know you will, Matthew," he said.

This was our procedure for over twenty hours during a three-day period. I was given a small celllike room with a chair and a desk on which one volume at a time was placed. Each volume contained handwritten letters from parish priests and traveling Jesuits.

One was from a Jesuit who had accompanied a clan leader on a cattle drive to Limerick in 1668, before the English forces and colonists had taken their land. It and others described the "wild Irish on the north coast."

One was an account of a shipwrecked Spanish seaman who spent six months with these "wild Irish." A Jesuit, concerned about the old pagan ways of the native Irish, did a bit of spying. He gave a detailed description of the traveling teachers who instructed the young men in Irish and clan history, the Brehon Laws, horsemanship, and weaponry.

Having these accounts, I envisioned Ireland in 1670 to 1690, how young Hogan grew up from about age ten to manhood, how he earned the reputation as the best horseman in Ireland, how he became known as the Galloping Hogan.

My spirits soared when I found one collection of quill penned letters which had frequent references to the Hogans of Ardcrony. The language was antique, but to me beautiful and thrilling. The writer was an Italian priest, one of many sent by the Vatican to report on the condition of Roman Catholics in southeastern Ireland. He wrote:

The O'Hogans were an ancient and hospitable clan that held ample and fair possessions in the province of Munster, and who, in ancient times, adorned the See of Killaloe with four very learned and exemplary prelates: namely, Matthew O'Hogan, who succeeded to this Bishopric in the reign of Henry III in the year of Our Lord 1267 and performed many acts of popular charity, died in the year 1281, and was buried in Limerick in the Convent of the Dominican Friars; . . . Maurice O'Hogan, who governed this See with peculiar zeal and charity upwards of sixteen years and died in 1298 and was buried in his own church; Thomas O'Hogan, Canon of Killaloe, was consecrated Bishop in 1343 and died on the 30th of October, 1354, being buried among his ancestors at Nenagh; Richard O'Hogan succeeded to this See in 1525 and was in 1539 transferred to Clanmacnoise. This ancient family was represented in 1559 by Edward O'Hogan, high sherriff of the county of Clare.

He later described the people he saw in Ireland: "The men are tall, possessing incredible strength, very fleet afoot. They endure hardship with indescribable patience; all are accustomed to the use of arms."

He expressed surprise over the literary pursuits of the men he met. Then he described the women:

> The women excel in grace and beauty to a remarkable degree. They exhibit comeliness with singular modesty and charm to display complete openmindedness and to engage in social intercourse without provoking any comment or misgiving. They dress themselves in a fashion which in some respects resembles that of the French. They wear cloaks that reach to the ankles; the cloaks are adorned with pendant tassels, tufted like human hair, the tassels being attached to the garment in place of a collar so that it resembles a pallium. The headdress is a linen fillet almost in the manner of the Greeks, so their natural beauty shone forth. All are married with large families. The children are naturally beautiful, of good stature and health; they are mostly black- or auburn-haired with a white and rosy complexion.

I was getting mild shocks as I read on:

> The Clan O'Hogan lands, bordered on the west by the river Shannon, are not the largest in the Dalcassians. The lands of the O'Kennedys, to the north and east, are more extensive, as are the lands of the O'Briens, the MacMahons, and other ancient Dalcassian clans. Much O'Hogan land passed maternally to the O'Briens with whom they have common ancestry, and to neighboring families, through marriage. Nonetheless, the O'Hogan clan is very strategically located for agriculture, defense, hunting, fishing and recreation, and its close access to the counties of Clare, Limerick and Kerry. There are long periods of peace, but because the soul of Ireland was born in the breast of violent, turbulent, pagan people, the clans have fought with some regularity over land, cattle, horses and family honor. This was regrettably true between the O'Hogans and the O'Kennedys, whose lands adjoined. Previous conflicts between the O'Hogans and the O'Kennedys were resolved by individual and group battles, with periods of peace in between, generally promoted by family chieftains who reminded them they were of the same blood through ancient marriages. The worst of these battles, however, could not be forgotten. It transpired that in 1599 a band of O'Hogans and O'Kennedys fought during midweek; an O'Hogan was ambushed and killed. The dead

O'Hogan was a favorite of his uncle, Father John O'Hogan, prior of Lorrha. At mass the following Sunday, during his sermon, with O'Kennedys in the congregation, Father O'Hogan castigated the O'Kennedys for the event. Enraged, the O'Kennedys left the church and waited outside. They then attacked and killed the Father Superior of the Dominican Monastery of Lorrha. The greatly-loved John O'Hogan was mourned and buried on a hill overlooking the Monastery he loved and served so well.

I took a very long pause after reading that. This was undoubtedly the very kind of time bomb of which the trustees of the monastery had lived in fear.

The ancestors of the late President of the United States had killed the father superior of a famous monastery in 1599—on the front steps of the church!

Now I had an ethical problem. Could I use that story? I could not, under my agreement with the head of the monastery. In any case, I decided to ask him directly.

I was to have my next shock within minutes—the Italian priest wrote about some peaceful times and areas that were relatively unaffected around 1500. But, he reported:

One hundred years later, the ancient Ireland was no more; the Dalcassian clans had been driven off their lands, with the majority of their warriors and chiefs killed or maimed. The surviving O'Hogan men, women and children fled to the mountains and wooded hills of Slieve Felim and Slieve Aughty, where they survived all manner of hardships and oppression by the occupying forces of King Henry VIII.

The scourge of the O'Hogans and the other uprooted clans was the brutal and sadistic Earl of Rosse, sent to Ireland by Henry VIII after he broke with the Roman Catholic Church over his divorce demands. His instructions to Rosse were to destroy the Roman Catholic Church and the great clans. Rosse's reward was a gift of the O'Hogan lands along the Shannon. The family name of the Earl of Rosse was Parsons. To this day they occupy the land ruthlessly ripped from the Clan Hogan. I indulged myself with some wild thoughts about launching a lawsuit in a Dublin court to regain the Hogan land. Then I had the sobering thought that I might win the suit. Then what would I do?

The report of the Italian priest, a most scholarly man capable of writing in English, ended with:

Only the blessing of the heavily wooded hills and mountains of Slieve Felim and Slieve Aughty saved the O'Hogans. The soldiers of England were invulnerable in their camps and in the defenses of the level ground. Their superior weapons and numbers made it impossible for the Irish to fight pitched battles. There was no Irish army, but gradually small irregular forces were organized. They were patterned after the bands of ancient China. Word of these bands and their tactics was smuggled into Ireland by soldiers and officers who had left Ireland to serve in the armies of France and Spain. The tactics, created by a Chinese rebel leader, were expressed eight hundred years earlier in simple terms: "The people are the water. The warriors are the fish, living in the water."

The Italian priest did not use the word *Rapparees,* either because he had never heard it or because it had not yet been coined.

The next long letter, this one written by an Irish Jesuit with a lovely, easy-to-read script, described how self-sufficient the clan families were in their mountain homes. The exception, he explained, was the cattle market in Limerick. He wrote:

There was no need of other markets in 1670. Each family grew its own food, eggs, vegetables, potatoes and bread. The herds and flocks provided delicious bacon, lamb and beef. The women made their clothes. Tea and tobacco, metals and smooth fabrics were brought in by foreigners. Except for the cattle market in Limerick, the people of East Clare—the O'Briens, the Kennedys, the MacLysaghts and the Hogans—were oriented toward Tipperary and Waterford, east, rather than toward the western tribes, whom they mistrusted.

Their speech and accents were the same as the "Tip" and Waterford people, as were their sports and dances. But for the cattle market, Limerick was heaven on earth.

. . . All the men and boys over ten participated in the cattle market. It mattered greatly, though, if the family was buying or selling. Unencumbered by a herd, the objective was to get to Limerick as fast as possible. With a herd, the objective was safety and speed. The men guarded and guided the herds from behind and alongside. The boys were essential; they raced ahead as "stop gaps" where the hedges along the trail had broken down, and at side roads, to keep the cattle from straying. When a beast did stray, it was the job of the older boys to chase it and get it back in the herd.

The relay system, utilizing the limited number of horses and donkeys, had been developed eons before; boys had to keep moving, the animals had to be rested. The older boys would start on horses and donkeys an hour before the herd. They would ride hard until the animals showed tiredness, then they would tie up the animals in a ditch and trot on. The next rider, arriving in an hour or so, would take a fresh mount, leaving the tired one to rest.

The Jesuit traced the cattle drive all the way to Limerick, finishing his letter with his description of the recreation of the boys, once freed of their clan duties.

He recounted what pranks he had seen: boys stuffing straw into the chimney of a house, backing up the smoke, sending its inhabitants streaming out coughing, teary-eyed; throwing straw spears at the young men walking out with young ladies (under the eyes of their chaperones), knowing their victims couldn't give chase; leaping out of the shadows screaming like banshees at older, often-inebriated men.

More good fortune came with a letter from an Irish priest whose principal nonreligious interest was horses. His report, obviously directed toward the Vatican since all Irishmen would know what he knew about horses, read:

The horse was in Ireland before we were. It was a small horse, it had to be. It lived in Connemara, where the land was coarse and rocky. Bigger horses came to Ireland with a Celtic tribe known as La Téne people. They had them tied to chariots, and rode and fought in these. They won enough battles to convince all others, and soon most clans had men in chariots, though the best warriors fought on horseback.

The Fianna Clan ruled this part of Ireland until St. Patrick came about a thousand years ago. They rode, hunted, fought on horseback, then raced their fastest horses against each other.

Pictures of these horses were drawn by the monks in monasteries long, long ago. Many of the pictures were of peacetime. These pictures show Irishmen riding bareback; in the horse's mouth was a metal bit the horse couldn't bite through.

I felt like a schoolboy now, learning:

Somewhere about three hundred years after St. Patrick came to Ireland, everything concerning horses became part of the Brehon Law and the customs. Clansmen of any rank had to learn to ride. All the sons were taught to ride very early. Horses and saddles became a kind of money. Tribute was paid in horses and saddles.

He described the various breeds:

The Cashel, Ireland's greatest breed, was developed at Cashel, hence the name. It is the biggest horse in Ireland, but not only strong. It is fast, and has great endurance. It has a noble, long head and unusually long forelegs and very high withers. That is the secret of its great starting speed.

The smaller horses are part Spanish. Most of the big grey horses are part Arabian. They are fast and have great heart. Their bones are light, though, so they can't be used in very rocky country. The horses up north, in Donegal and Connemara, are crossbreeds of the Connemara pony. They are small, but very quick and gentle with children.

Then some wonder crept into the priest's report as he wrote that he had learned one of the secrets of the Rapparees. Somewhere in the past, one of the first Rapparees had trained his Cashel in such a way that he could leap on his rapidly accelerating horse by holding onto the horse's left ear and mane. When the horse bounded forward, the Rapparee would use the momentum to leap onto the horse's back in emergencies.

In an unusual corroboration about the way they lived, there were two letters about "the wild Irish" of the northern coastal area, one from a priest, one from a shipwrecked sailor. The sailor wrote:

It was north, and on the coast above angry ocean, bashing against the most rugged coastline I have seen. All the houses were little more than shelters made of straw and rushes. The people were large and strong, but more than that they were fast and nimble as the roe deer that bounded through the scrubby, rock-covered hills. At first, I had difficulty keeping up with the children, much less the adults, who ran among, around and over rocks and boulders with what appeared to be recklessness. But not one fell or even stumbled.

I wore their clothes, made of coarse goat skin. I even let my hair grow like theirs, long in back, bangs in front, right down to my eyebrows.

Each evening I gathered rushes as they did, sleeping on a springy, fragrant bed of them covered with goatskin blankets. I ate one meal a day—bread, cheese, a powdered meal and sour milk, and occasionally meat. The women were the tallest, handsomest I had ever seen. They wore a single long slipover and a cloak which reached almost to the ground. The men played wild tunes on carved wooden flutes and goatskin bagpipes at night. What fascinated me most were the slings and bow and arrows with which they hunted and (I heard) fought. There were no battles while I was there, but there was daily hunting for birds, game and deer. Their accuracy was astounding with both the bow and arrow and with each of the three slings they used. One they carried in hand, for most likely use. Another was worn as a head band. The third, for long range, circled the waist as a girdle. I was amazed as the men would run at tremendous speeds, leap to a halt and speed a sling shot at a deer, a bird or a ground animal with deadly accuracy. The stones, perfectly round, ranged from plum pit to orange size.

The Spanish sailor marveled at his acceptance by these "wild Irish." One of the older warriors said that "in olden times the blood of toads and vixens was mixed with sea water and hardened to make the sling shot." He felt he was perhaps being spoofed when another told him, "My grandfather used the brains of defeated, decapitated enemies, mixed with lime as weapons and trophies."

There were then many unproductive hours as I peered at page after page of sad, grim, horrifying reports of priests and Jesuits who were caught by the English, some tried and imprisoned or executed, others summarily killed. Dragging priests behind galloping horses was a favored pastime, but the most brutal death, by hanging, drawing, and quartering, was reserved for the captured Jesuits.

My final hours were startlingly productive, as I began to read multiple reports on the Rapparees from different priests and Jesuits.

One priest wrote that "at age sixteen young men, strong, very fleet afoot, and already able horsemen, joined one of the four or five bands of Rapparees in the south of Ireland." Near the lands of the Hogans, the White Sergeant was the most famous. He was elected leader when the Rapparee he replaced rode in an insane fury into an English troop that had killed his family in a reprisal raid. The man inflicted great damage in his blood lust, but fell fatally wounded. His band felt he wanted release from life.

The new leader ordered that no names henceforth be used. He had served in the regular army as a sergeant, and so he pinned an outsize white feather on his Rapparee's hat and announced that he would from then on be known as the White Sergeant—"I want the bloody bastards to always know where *I* am."

He had a controlled ferocity, which made him deadly as a leader as well as a man. At a critical point in a raid, whenever possible, he would emerge from his command place emitting a blood-curdling shriek and gallop straight at the leader of the opposing force, saber flashing, face contorted, teeth bared, white feather jutting skyward. His men would become like demons, attacking with superhuman force. Often the enemy leader would flee. If he stood he died.

As the White Sergeant became older, he knew his time of death or abdication approached. He kept his keen eye on the younger Rapparees for signs of strength and intelligence. He received regular reports of the tracking abilities, the weapons, and the horsemanship of the young Rapparees. A terrible test would have to be passed by the most promising young prospect for leadership.

To pass the test, he would have to learn the most carefully guarded secret of the Rapparees. He was ordered to ride out of camp at dusk with four older men. They stopped outside the camp, cut down some strong young saplings, and carried them to a section of bog that ran along the firm road. One of the older Rapparees, standing on a kind of raft, drove a long stake into the bog again and again as the raft was pulled across the bog by the straining men.

When he found what he sought, the men stopped the raft, and the group leader explained to the fledgling Rapparee what he was to do. It must have been a dreadful shock. A large piece of tweed material, made like a sack, was brought forth. The candidate stepped into it, as he had been told. The sack was well oiled and came to the top of his head. The saplings were crossed at the top like a teepee, and a crude pulley was installed with a rope tied to the sack in which he stood and looped around his shoulders.

The leader whispered, "There is a firm footing about your height down. You'll be lowered into the bog feet first. We'll cover your head from here. The sack will protect you from the wet and cold, and in fact, lad, you'll be warm very soon. We'll be back for you, God willing, in about three hours." And so it was.

The teepeelike sapling structure was inclined out over the bog; the scout was lifted up, then lowered straight down into the soft muck. He knew the worst terror of his young life as he sank deeper and deeper into the foul-smelling bog. When he was about to say his final act of contrition, his feet reached firm ground and his descent stopped. The rope was retrieved. A clump of brush, indistinguishable from the bog, was thrust out on a long, light sapling until it covered his head.

His comrades left, and he prayed. True as he was told, he stayed dry; then his body warmth, unable to escape, warmed his cell and himself. He hadn't needed to be told not to move unnecessarily. What he had been told—and what had motivated him to accept this challenge—was that this was the secret method used by the Rapparees to spy on the traveling troops of English soldiers as they camped in various spots throughout the forests, which were usually dotted with similar bogs. The lookout would stay thus submerged in a nearby bog, disguised by the brush over his head, but able to hear the goings on and words of the English. Thus English plans and moves were known to the Rapparees in a way which to the English was incomprehensible.

True to their words, his fellows returned after three hours. They lifted the scout out of the bog victorious over one of the grimmest experiences faced by these grim men. Such were the circumstances out of which the Galloping Hogan emerged. To become a chief of a band of Rapparees tested the whole man, for leaders were selected by the men they led—men who knew well that their lives, their families' lives, and their country's life depended on the quality of their leaders.

It is known that members of each band of Rapparees, holding their wicked daggers like crosses to their lips, intoned a pledge to their chiefs: "I will follow you *to the death.*"

There was one brief reference to the Galloping Hogan among the papers I read that afternoon, and several to his headquarters and hide-away known as Hogan's Glen. I vowed to find Hogan's Glen. At the end of the third day, I met for the last time with the abbot. I must have looked troubled, for he asked, "I hope it is only because of your leaving tonight. Is there anything else I can do?"

I told him of my discovery about the ancestors of the late President Kennedy, how potentially useful it would be to me for my book, but that I felt it was impossible to use it under the terms of our pact unless he gave me permission.

"Yes," he said, "that could be traced back here if that is the only written record—but," he brightened visibly, "I cannot believe such an event would not be recorded elsewhere. I mean, the killing of a father superior, even as far back as 1600 . . ."

"Well, where is Lorrha, the Dominican Monastery?" I asked. "I never have seen the name on a map."

"Oh," he replied quickly, "it's a famous ruin, north and east of Portumna, at the north end of Lough Derg."

"Well, Father, let's leave it this way. I'll go to Lorrha, check everything, even the tombstones. If there is no other record I'll forget I ever read it."

"Oh, the old church was burned down hundreds of years ago," the priest said. "But records must exist. Even if they don't exist in Ireland, they may in the Vatican."

I had a deep, dreamless sleep that night, awakening at dawn, around 5:30. I felt oddly calm and expectant. I was going as close to the ancient Hogans as I had ever been, to the monastery where John Hogan had lived and died—murdered—and had been buried. The dawn was spectacularly beautiful as I started my drive to Lorrha.

I expected no hitchhikers that early, so I had made no decision on whether to pick anyone up when I spied a spindly, forlorn male ahead, speaking the kind of body language that shouted neglect and desperation. I was past him when I decided to stop. I looked back through the rearview mirror and saw the most eerily comical sight in memory.

The figure exploded into gyrating action. His red hair flew wildly, his arms and legs pumped, it seemed, without communication. His coattails flapped; his flared trousers swirled; his noise preceded him. He wore thick-soled shoes that made him sound like a flamenco dancer in heat. He yanked open the car door and belted out a few sentences that told me I was to be graced with one of the rarest birds in captivity, a young "Dublin Jack," the Irish nickname for a born-and-bred Dubliner.

Nothing I've attempted in this book rivals this endeavor to interpret my Dublin Jack in writing alone. The speech, the words, the cadences were extraordinary. The use of "you know," which comes out "ya new," far exceeds that found in the inarticulate segment of young people in the United States, but it is not a product of laziness or punctuation. "Ya new" can be said in a dozen ways, with the accent on "ya" or on "new." A rising inflection means one sentiment, a falling another. Dublin Jacks mainly live by their wits, which are considerable, as I hope this episode will attest.

"Are ya in Ireland on vacation?" he asked.

I explained my work in research. I said I was making a run to Lorrha, where there was a famous monastery ruin.

He said, "Lorrha is grand, particularly since it's so close to Cavan . . ."

Just that. I had to ask, "Cavan? County Cavan? What's so special about Cavan?"

"Well, ya new," said my companion, "ya haven't seen Ireland until ya've seen Cavan, ya new."

"Is it like Tipperary?" I asked innocently.

"Not atall, ya new," he replied. "Cavan, ya new, is called the land of lakes and rocks. Thousands of lakes, ya new." He continued his eulogy as I headed toward Lorrha and, incidentally, Cavan. It was at Cavan I realized the con. My Dublin Jack was a salesman of plastic shopping bags, mainly rejects for minor errors in printing. He sold them cheap, to stores, warehouses, and farmers. He asked me if I'd mind if he "stopped a minute to see a feller." He came back with a broad smile and an order for bags from the town grocer. I knew then that he was on a territorial selling trip, without a car or a bike. By this time I had smiled, chuckled, and laughed aloud dozens of times as he reeled off stories about the Dublin slums in which he lived.

That his hype, successful, was more than worth my expense of time and miles was obvious from my sincere regret at leaving him off in Cavan. I drove on to Lorrha, still smiling and chuckling at his stories, his absurd appearance, and his overabundant sense of the humor of life.

Then, less than forty miles from Scariff, my ultimate destination, I saw the tiny road sign to Lorrha, a town so small it didn't appear on my map. I screeched to a halt, backed up, and headed down the road to the town. I felt somewhat disembodied. At Lorrha, there were two signs: one pointing to the Dominican Priory, the other to Saint Rudyhan's Church. Both were ruins, but in back of the abbey was a small new church. One entrance was through a graveyard. Some stones were new, some so old that the inscriptions were almost completely worn away.

I spied two workmen taking down an old stone wall. They were startled to see me, but reacted with Irish friendliness. I said, "I'm on my way to Scariff to see the Hogans, my mother's people."

"Lots of Hogans around here," said one, pointing to the graves, grinning broadly.

"Some old records I've seen say that a John O'Hogan was prior of the Dominican Monastery here at Lorrha," I prompted.

"You may find more than that," the other old man said with a secret smile. "You see Father Ryan. He knows more than any man alive about Lorrha." The men pointed, gnarl-handed, to Father Ryan's house, less than one hundred yards away. It was a charming little white cottage, with a lawn, flowering trees and bushes, surrounded by fencing to keep the cattle and sheep out. I drove in. The greeting was from the housekeeper, who told me that the Father was at a funeral and would be back about "half one."

I wandered around the ruins and the graveyard and peered futilely at the old stones, unable to see anything on the older ones or any reference to Hogans on the newer.

Father Ryan, when I saw him about "half one," did more for me than simply confirm that John O'Hogan was prior of Lorrha. He asked, "Did you visit the church?" I said I had.

"Did you notice the newest wall plaque, the one to MacLysaght?"

I nodded and almost said, "Aye." "Well," continued Father Ryan, "when I first got here, I was interested in the MacLysaght family. I noticed a gravestone in the floor right below the wall plaque. I assumed it was a MacLysaght grave, but then I saw it was carved in the old Celtic manner around the perimeter and, of course, was much, much older than the plaque."

"Uh-oh," I said, sensing what might be coming.

"Yes, Matthew," Father Ryan continued, "I got down on these old arthritic knees and traced the Latin inscription. It was the gravestone of John O'Hogan."

"My God," I gasped, "that is the first piece of physical evidence of the O'Hogans I know about."

"Matthew," Father Ryan said, "there is more, much, much more. I want to help you, for there is much more about the O'Hogans I've found for reasons having nothing to do with them, really."

"Tell me, please," I pleaded, "I'm bursting with curiosity."

"I decided that this parish needed a bigger, better church, so I sought permission to start raising funds. The bishop gets many requests, some better justified than others. It's frankly a bit of a selling job. I dug into the records here and sought the help of some of the families that had been here longer than they could remember. Are you ready for this?"

"I'm ready," I understated, in a manner painfully controlled.

"During the thirteenth, fourteenth, and fifteenth centuries, there were three bishops of Killaloe, all O'Hogans."

"Father," I interrupted, "now you're in for a shock. There were *four* bishops of Killaloe who were O'Hogans . . . but I can't tell you how I know that."

"Were there, now?" Father Ryan asked. "And do you know about Ballyhogan and the ring fort there?"

"It's mentioned in MacLysaght's book as the clan headquarters."

"How would you account for the fact that the Hogans were spread over so much of Tipperary, Clare, and Limerick?" I asked.

"Well, now, that is simple enough in retrospect," Father Ryan said. "The Hogans, you see, were what could be called an ecclesiastical family, originally very strong supporters and defenders of the Catholic Church. In addition to those who became priests and bishops, many were sent as sextons to new parishes in the general area."

"And *bally*, Father, means . . . ?" I asked.

"The word *bally* in ancient times meant town. So Ballyhogan would be the Hogan clan village. You've got to get there, Matthew. You can still see the round earthen fort they used in those times against surprise attacks and to keep their cattle, sheep, goats, and horses under control."

The village of Étretat north of Le Havre, Normandy, France. This magnificent coastline would have been the first heights seen by Patrick Sarsfield, Lawrence Mahon, and Michael Hogan and the Wild Geese, as they reached the Normandy coast. (Courtesy French Government Tourist Office)

Sarah Jane Hogan, mother of author—daughter of Domenic Hogan wounded at Kilmallock, County Limerick, in 1867.

The ford of the Shannon at Ballyvalley, roughly north of Killaloe Bridge. The Shannon in 1690 was much narrower. Its present width is the result of the Power Station Dam erected in modern times. (Photo by Liam Hogan)

Labbadiha Bridge from the narrow trail leading down to Hogan's Glen. Dense foliage screened the glen from view and muffled all sounds. (Photo by Liam Hogan)

Sarsfield's Rock, the perpetual symbol of the ride to Ballyneety, led by the Galloping Hogan, in August 1690. The boulder in the foreground is one of scores flung about the area by the explosion of the artillery train of King William of England. (Photo by Liam Hogan)

Near the top of Sarsfield's Rock visitors can rest and read the brief account of Sarsfield's Ride, beautifully hand carved in the old manner. (Photo by Liam Hogan)

The Treaty Stone on which the Treaty of Limerick was signed. (Bord Failte photo)

Author near middle of the Killaloe Bridge, across the Shannon, joining the west and east banks of the river at Killaloe and Ballina. The monument honors four young men killed on this spot by the British Auxiliaries. (Photo by Liam Hogan)

The castle at the Rock of Cashel, County Tipperary. One rumor has it that the Galloping Hogan was captured and executed by the British in the courtyard of this castle. The greatest horse in Ireland, known as the Cashel, was bred in this vicinity. (Bord Failte photo)

Landscape typical of the area in Tipperary over which Sarsfield's Band was led by the Galloping Hogan. (Bord Failte photo)

Permanent sign, in Gaelic and English, marking Hogan's Glen. (Photo by Liam Hogan)

MARCAÍOCHT AN tSÁIRSÉALAIGH

Do réir an tseanchais, is anseo ag Droichead Leaba Daibhche (nó Gleann an Ógánaigh) , ar oíche an 10ú Lúnasa 1690, a casadh buíon Rapairí ar Phádraig Sáirséal agus a 600 marcach. Threoraigh Ó hÓgáin, ceannaire na Rapairí, an Sáirséalach agus a mharcshlua go Baile an Fhaoitigh, chun gunnaí móra Rí Liam a scrios.

SARSFIELD'S RIDE

According to tradition it was here at Labbadiha Bridge (or Hogan's Glen) , on the night of August 10th, 1690 that Patrick Sarsfield and his 600 troopers were joined by a party of Raparees. It was Galloping O Hogan, the leader of the Raparees, who led Sarsfield and his men to Ballyneety to blow up the Williamite siege train.

he breathtaking cliffs of Mohar in the old Dalcassian territory. (Bord Failte photo)

Typical area in Ardcrony, where the ancient O'Hogans held clan lands during the 16th, 15th, 14th, 13th centuries, and earlier. (Bord Failte photo)

"The Burren," in County Clare, dominated by the Rapparees, where the English dared not go. (Bord Failte photo)

The countryside of Moura in Portugal unchanged from the days when General André Miguel Hogan commanded the cavalry and organized the raid that saved Campo Maior during the last battle of the Peninsular War in 1712. (Photo courtesy Centro de Turismo de Portugal)

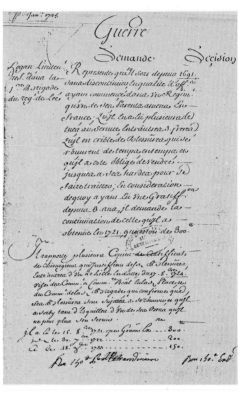

One of the more than thirty documents about the Hogans gotten from the military archives of the Portuguese army at the Tombo in Lisbon. These documents were so fragile that they could not be copied. The author had them photographed with special equipment.

One of the thirteen copies of the original documents written in 1706, about Jean Hogan, promoted from lieutenant to captain. These documents were secured by Count Patrick de Mac-Mahon, with whom the author shares a common ancestor. The originals are in the military archives of the Bibliothèque Nationale at Vincennes, outside Paris, France.

A self-portrait of João Navarro Hogan, the grandson of Ricardo Possolo Hogan. His work is displayed in the Gulbenkian museums in Lisbon and Paris, where he now lives.

MEMORIALS

OF

JOHN HOGAN,

The Great Irish Sculptor.

Born October, 1800.   Died March, 1857.

By BENMORE.

John Hogan, a member of the Virtuosi de Parthenon in Rome. Considered by many to be the best sculptor in western Europe, England, and Ireland during the 1840s and 1850s.

The late John Fitzgerald Kennedy and Matthew J. Culligan-Hogan in the oval office of the White House. The author was, at that time, chairman and president of the Curtis Publishing Company. (Photo by Ollie Atkins, official White House photographer)

"This is spectacular, Father," I applauded. "Would you like to celebrate with me with a jar?"

"No, Matthew, I'm a teetotaler," Father Ryan said sadly. "You know, the Irish relate hospitality and friendship with drink and food. Once it's known that you drink *at* all, you must drink *with* all. On some days, I might visit ten families and therefore be plied with at least ten drinks, and the vision of a man of the cloth, especially one my age, intoxicated five days out of the week seems to me rather uninspiring for my parishioners. But I have here what we call the priest's bottle. You'll have a jar here with me?"

And so I did, a healthy glass of Power's Irish.

"Now, Matthew, I'm going to tell you something which *must* be useful to you in some way—humor, publicity—or other. Between what we know of the O'Hogans in the thirteenth century and King Henry VIII's break with the church, they held a group of castles, with churches and abbeys, around Ardcrony in this part of Tipperary and extending into Clare and Limerick. The men, as faithful Roman Catholics, were killed in battle, and their survivors were driven off their land. The present Earl of Rosse is the direct descendant of the favorite of Henry VIII, and it was he who was given the O'Hogan land. The family name was . . .," he paused for effect, "Parsons. In recent times a lady of the Armstrong-Jones family married a Parsons."

I reacted with great surprise and glee, so as not to spoil his fun. I could have shouted. Now I was off the hook with the monastery about the Armstrong-Jones clue. I said, "You mean Antony Armstrong-Jones, who married Princess Margaret of England, is related by marriage to the blackguards who stole the O'Hogan lands?"

"Exactly, Matthew. One whole generation of the male O'Hogans was practically destroyed. The survivors fled to the hills until the children grew old enough to fight for King James in 1689."

I grew serious then, and prodded him further. "Father Ryan, another story I heard, and again I can't tell you from whom, is that the Hogans and Kennedys had a family feud, and . . ."

Here he interrupted. "That they did. In fact, the monastery records state that Father John O'Hogan, the prior of Lorrha, was killed on the very steps of his church—by O'Kennedys."

I did let out a yip at this. Now I could tell the story with no ethical restraints.

I very nearly got drunk that night celebrating my discoveries at Lorrha with John Guilfoyle and the O'Beirn lads in Scariff. When I drink too much, I can get fey, and sometime during the night, after a thundering rendition of the "Clare Brigade," I remember saying that I was "going to change my name to Culligan-Hogan and sue that Parsons family to get back the O'Hogan land."

The next morning I rested, partly to recover from my hangover and partly to review what astonishing luck I had had as a result of visiting and knowing Father Henry. I had gone to him looking for John Hogan, the sculptor of 1840, and in addition I had found four family bishops, a father superior killed by the ancestors of a late President of the United States, and the thieving of my ancestral land. And, most important, I found two new friends—Father Ryan, pastor of Saint Rudyhan's Church, and the abbot in Dalcassia.

6 🍀 The Ride to Ballyneety

Come ride with me across the Shannon,
To the sounding of the drum
And we'll blow the enemy siege train
To the land of kingdom come.

"Ballad of the Galloping Hogan"

I RACED back to Dublin, to Father Henry, to report on my success and to tell him that I could now empathize with the Galloping Hogan and the Wild Geese. He waved off my thanks and delightedly reported progress on the first name of the Galloping Hogan. He had been in touch with Desmond Rush, author of the "Tattler's Corner" in the *Irish Independent*, a large newspaper published in Dublin and distributed all over Ireland. Desmond Rush had interviewed me about my quest. One reader who described himself as being over ninety years old had written to Rush, stating the Galloping Hogan was Michael Hogan of Doon.

That was direct support of my mother's belief that Michael was his first name. Father Henry noticed that I wasn't jumping for joy—there was no Michael or M. Hogan in the Portuguese military records that I knew about yet.

Father Henry wasn't dismayed. He speculated that the Hogans might have adopted other names, Portuguese names. "God be with you," he said, as I left full of enthusiasm for the actual writing now ahead, intent on answering the question which towered above the rest: Why did Patrick Sarsfield, a mature, experienced military leader, surrounded by untrustworthy peers and superiors, put his life, the lives of 500 officers and

men, the city of Limerick, and in fact the entire cause of Roman Catholic Ireland in the hands of the Galloping Hogan? For that is precisely
what he did. The historical circumstances are thoroughly documented.

Patrick Sarsfield, enraged by the flaccid leadership of James II and
near desperation after the defeat in the north, was quoted as saying, "If
Limerick dies, we all die." His passion was not matched by the political
leader of the Irish, the Duke of Tyrconnell and the commander of the
French forces Count de Lauzun. They held a council of war in early
August 1690, urging the surrender of Limerick to King William, whose
army encircled the city.

Count de Lauzun was particularly àdamant. He scoffed at Sarsfield's
plan of defense, saying, "The walls of Limerick could be battered down
with roasted apples." Sarsfield rallied the Limerick council of war. The
Tyrconnell-Lauzun plan was refused. De Lauzun skulked away from Limerick, taking the French soldiers and badly needed artillery with him.
He fled to Galway and embarked for France.

Lord Tyrconnell appointed King James's bastard son, the Duke of
Berwick, commander in chief, disdaining Sarsfield, who was still only
a colonel of dragoons. Tyrconnell and Berwick tried to isolate Sarsfield,
but the military commander of Limerick, French General Boisseleaux,
properly judged him the best hope of the successful defense of Limerick.

King William, knowing of the crumbling walls and the defection of
Count de Lauzun, "summoned the town," the phrase that demanded
surrender. He was defiantly rebuffed, given the seventeenth-century
equivalent of "Nuts!" He ordered an immediate attack. It was repulsed
with heavy casualties, his commanders citing inadequate artillery. King
William bellowed for speed from his artillery siege train which was lum-
bering north along the roads from Cashel toward Limerick.

Fate took a hand with the appearance of a defector from the Williamite army at Sarsfield's camp. His news confirmed the reports coming to
Sarsfield from the Galloping Hogan, some of whose Rapparees were
scouting the massive siege train, the biggest ever to enter Ireland.

In our times it sounds somewhat like a tin soldiers' display, but during
the Williamite-Jacobite war, when a big battle might involve 10,000
men *on both sides*, it was mammoth. It contained: 6 24-pounders, 2 18-
pounders, 8 brass ordnance of 18 inches, 1 mortar of 18 inches with 30
shells and 15 carcasses, 6 tin boats of three sections each, 800 balls for
18-pounder, 120 barrels of powder, 1,600 barrels of matches, 500 hand
grenades, 3,000 tools, 94 wool bags, 12 casks of biscuits, a quantity of

all sorts of timber, a "gynn" or crane, block wagons, limbers and spare gun carriages, 153 wagons drawn by 400 draft horses, all under the command of Captain Pulteney.

With that artillery not only would King William be invincible in battle but, with Limerick in ruins, the Irish would have lost any bargaining power.

Patrick Sarsfield, trained under King Louis XIV's military genius, Luxembourg, knew his moment of glory or death had come. The artillery siege train was approaching via Ballyneety in Tipperary, the logical staging area for crossing the River Shannon. There it would be temporarily vulnerable.

So Sarsfield sends a message
To a fearless Rapparee—

The Galloping Hogan.

That much of the story of Patrick Sarsfield and the desperate condition of Ireland we know as historically supportable fact.

The Galloping Hogan's part in the Ballyneety raid and its profound success is also clearly supported by ballads, songs, and poems, as well as some factual history.

By any standards Sarsfield's Ride to Ballyneety, guided by the Galloping Hogan, was a heroic feat. While the distance as the magpie flies was less than fifteen miles, the Galloping Hogan led the troop almost ninety miles north, then east, then south, and finally west, to avoid the spies and Williamite supporters who lived in and around Limerick.

He led them out the north gate of Limerick in the opposite direction of Ballyneety, fording the Shannon River where Lough Derg joins it above the town of Ballina. Once across the Shannon, he led them east past the village of Shallee and then south, with the Silvermine Mountains shielding the mounted band from observers.

He kept them moving south, resting at Ballyhourigan Wood, then through the foothills of the Slievefelim Mountains, past the village of Doon, straight south to Monard, where they paused and received scout reports. They were less than five miles from Ballyneety.

The final scout reports brought grim smiles to the faces of the Galloping Hogan and Sarsfield. The Galloping Hogan had made the location of the 500 horses of the enemy his highest priority. Five hundred whinneying, grazing horses make a great deal of noise. Hogan would use

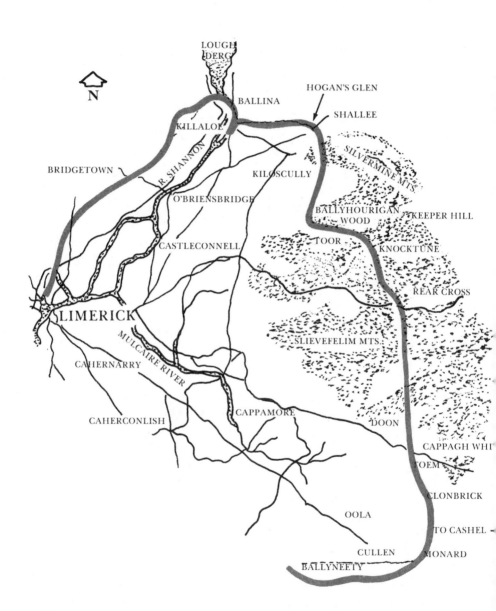

that noise to mask the sounds of Sarsfield's troopers, which had already been reduced to a minimum by coarse, burlap-type fabric covering the hooves of the horses.

A most significant strategic error of the commander of the artillery train was to ignore the ruins of Ballyneety Castle. One whole flank of the camp could have been shielded by the castle walls. Lookouts could have been posted on top. But he didn't take advantage of the castle, which lessened Sarsfield's chances of discovery and reduced his casualties.

Sarsfield and the Galloping Hogan did not know how close to absolute disaster they came. Despite all their precautions and the masking ride north and east, one Williamite supporter saw the ghostly band glide silently by his farmhouse. He didn't know precisely where they were going, but the size and silence of the band alerted him. He saddled his horse and rode directly to the main force of King William and attempted to get his report to him. He had an advantage of hours over the Galloping Hogan, who was using the circuitous route.

The officers of William of Orange, intoxicated by their victory over the Irish in the battles in the north, inexplicably delayed the introduction of the Williamite supporter, with the result that the king did not get the word until about eight or nine o'clock in the evening. However, it was early enough to have led to an ambush of the Galloping Hogan and the band of Sarsfield. King William sent orders to a nearby regiment of dragoons to join the artillery train at Ballyneety. By all standards the relief column of dragoons should have left for Ballyneety at about ten o'clock, arriving around midnight after a two-hour ride. For some unknown reason, the column did not leave its camp until one o'clock in the morning. The raid on the artillery train started at two o'clock, with Sarsfield's troopers entering the camp virtually undetected. One of Hogan's Rapparees, left behind temporarily for the reshoeing of his horse, met a woman trudging wearily in the direction of Ballyneety. She was the wife of a Williamite soldier. The Rapparee befriended her (perhaps even made the supreme sacrifice), and she gave him the password of the enemy camp. Ironically, the password was *Sarsfield*.

The Galloping Hogan was able to get the Sarsfield troop to the edge of the camp. The sentries, getting the password when they challenged the shadowy approaching figures, were dead before they hit the ground, and Sarsfield's men raged into the sleeping camp and killed most of the one hundred enemy guards.

Now Sarsfield was in his element. He bellowed orders in his best battlefield voice, ordering the guns into a circle, muzzles inward. They were then filled with gunpowder and the muzzles driven into the ground. All the excess powder, shells, carts, and supplies were put in the middle of the circle and a fast powder trail laid from the edge of the woods to the powder. Sarsfield ordered all the troopers into the woods, giving the Galloping Hogan the honor of lighting the fuse. One eyewitness account quoted Sarsfield as saying, "Now give it the match, O'Hogan, and we'll have an earthquake all our own."

And so it was. The powder trail sputtered, caught, and the flame raced toward the huge mound of powder in the middle of the circle. It exploded with an earthshaking roar, the loudest man-made sound ever heard in Ireland, and the sky lit up with a flash that could be seen from the walls of Limerick City. Then it was quiet for several seconds. Then there was another, a different, sound. The walls of the ruins of Bally-neety Castle tumbled down. A few more seconds of silence, and there came a still different sound. Tens of thousands of pieces of metal came whispering down through the trees, some of them hitting the cheering men and terrified horses, milling around in the woods.

By prearrangement a group of the troopers and Rapparees stampeded the enemy horses toward Limerick, both to confuse the pursuers and gain horses for construction work and food in a long siege. A rear guard also detached itself from the main force and grimly prepared for the worst. Hogan family history has it that there were Hogans in the rear guard, and some were wounded and a few killed.

The Galloping Hogan signaled the troop to follow him, and he took a different road back to Limerick, knowing that without Sarsfield and his best men and officers, Limerick would be taken even without the wrecked artillery train.

The scene at Limerick City can be easily imagined. The walls were filled with cheering Irish men and women. No one can ever know what Sarsfield and the Galloping Hogan said to each other when they parted outside the walls of Limerick. I believe the Galloping Hogan decided alone, or in consultation with Sarsfield, that the Galloping Hogan should disappear and all the Rapparees should be brought into the official army of Sarsfield for the final defense of Limerick City.

I have located nearly a dozen poems (like that of Knappogue Castle) and ballads that tell the story. Percy French added to the legend with this poem:

"GALLOPING" O'HOGAN

"They have sent for fresh artillery,
  The guns are on the way,
God help our hapless Limerick
  When dawns another day."
Thus speaks the gallant Sarsfield,
  As sadly he recalls
The famine and despair that lurk
  Behind those crumbling walls.

And yet one blow for freedom—
  One daring midnight ride:
And William may be humbled yet,
  For all his power and pride!
"Go! Bring to me 'The Galloper,'
  To Highway Hogan say,
'Tis Ireland hath need of him,
  And him alone to-day!"

The Soldier and the Highwayman
  Are standing face to face,
The fearless front, the eagle eye,
  In both of them we trace.
"Hogan! the night is dark and dread,
  Say can'st thou lead the way
To Keeper Mountain's black ravines
  Ere dawns another day?"

"Can the eagle find his eyrie?
  Can the fox forget his den?
I can lead ye as none other
  Of the Sliabh Cimalta men.
The black mare knows it blindfold,
  It's not by the stars she'll steer,
Ye'll be tonight on Keeper's height—
  And dawn will find ye here."

"Lead on!" and well he led them,
Though the Shannon ford ran deep,
And though the white-lipped flood ran fierce
Around O'Brien's Keep.
The sentinel on Killaloe
Looked out, but failed to see—
Six hundred silent horsemen ride
Behind the Rapparee.

That night by Ballyneety's towers
The English gunners lay.
King William's camp in safety lies
But twelve short miles away.
What need of further caution?
What Irish wolf would dare
To prowl around our camp tonight
So near the lion's lair?

An Irish wolf is near them now,
And Irish ears have heard
The chosen watchword for the night—
And "Sarsfield" was the word.
A tramp of horses: "Who's there? The Word?"
"Sarsfield!" the answer ran,
And then the sword smote downwards,
"Aye, and Sarsfield is the man!"

"To arms! The foe!" Too late, too late
Though Villier's vengeful blade
Is wet with Hogan's life-blood,
As he leads the ambuscade.
Then foot to foot, and hand to hand,
They battle round the guns,
Till victory declares itself
For Erin's daring sons.

"Oh! for those guns in Limerick now,
Placed on the city walls,
We'd bid King William breakfast
On his own black cannon balls!

It may not be—but trebly charged,
And filled with shot and shell,
They'll toll the robber's requiem,
And sound the soldier's knell."

Oh! sudden flash of blinding light!
Oh, hollow sounding roar!
Down history's page in Irish ears
It echoes evermore.
And Ballyneety's blackened tower
Still marks the famous place
Where Sarsfield staked his all to win
And won that midnight race!

In this poem is the first and only mention of the wounding of Hogan: "Though Villier's vengeful blade is wet with Hogan's life-blood. . . ."

Another eyewitness account reports that Sarsfield gave Hogan the honor of lighting the quick fuse to the powder trail that blew the artillery to smithereens. And a third says that the Galloping Hogan led Sarsfield and the dragoons back to Limerick. One family legend has it that several brothers and cousins of Hogan fought the rear guard action, which delayed the pursuers. Several were wounded; two were killed. If indeed Colonel Villiers, who led the pursuit, killed a Hogan, he did not kill the Galloping Hogan.

The route, now known as Sarsfield's Ride, is shown on the following map. I have driven and walked this route several times.

The curious relationship of William of Orange and James II was pithily illuminated in two direct quotes, one a request by King James to his son-in-law King William. (Yes, King William was married to Mary Stuart, daughter of King James.) It had to do with horses and carriages. Wrote James, "Howsoever the Prince of Orange uses me in other things, sure he will not refuse me the common civility of letting my horses and coaches come to me." When King William heard of the warm welcome and continuing deference of King Louis XIV and his court to James, he commented nastily, "When he has dragged that corpse around for three or four years, he will be as much embarrassed by him as I have been."

The Van Der Zees, both experienced English journalists (though he was born in Holland), had complete access to all the records of the campaign of King William in Ireland where he landed in 1690, with almost 36,000 troops and the largest artillery train ever seen in Ireland.

The combination of the superior manpower, the artillery, and the bold leadership of the English king gave him a solid victory in the daylong Battle of the Boyne. Afterward, the shattered Irish army fled toward Limerick.

When King William reached Limerick he was jubilant as he heard the report that the French troops had pulled out, taking their artillery with them. King William bit on an unripe victory.

The first major assault on Limerick was repulsed with heavy losses. The Van Der Zees wrote:

> The English found the siege of Limerick a miserable and depressing business. The rain poured steadily down, day by day, and the Irish gave them not a moment of rest, constantly harassing them with skirmishing parties. "They came so near we could hear them talk with the damned Irish brogue on their tongues," complained one Englishman bitterly. The Irish efforts were not confined to skirmishes; knowing the King's troops were short of ammunition, the one commander of brilliancy on the Irish side, General Sarsfield, took out on August 12th a raiding party to intercept the reinforcements that he had learned were on their way from Kilkenny. The English now paid for their contempt of their Irish opponents: this train of wagons loaded with urgently needed powder and several large guns was so lightly guarded that when Sarsfield swooped down on it in the dead of night he met almost no resistance. Both guns and powder were blown up and sixty of its English escort were killed.

The ride to Ballyneety, its startling success, was a romantic, victorious experience of the Irish in Ireland, making Patrick Sarsfield and the Galloping Hogan heroes.

I experienced the irresistible urge to replicate the ride to Ballyneety, if not on horseback, then by car and on foot, where necessary. I asked Colonel Hogan if he could accompany me. He agreed to do this; furthermore he communicated with Colonel Thomas Hartigan, officer commanding the Irish Army barracks in Limerick—known, naturally, as Sarsfield Barracks—telling him of my interest and passion to cover the route of the ride of the Galloping Hogan and Patrick Sarsfield. Colonel Hartigan made all the arrangements, even giving an assignment to two young cavalry officers to evaluate the ride from a military standpoint, and to draw a large-scale map of the entire area, with the route clearly marked.

We took off in early morning with the zeal of schoolboys, and in four hours we covered almost every foot of the ride to Ballyneety. The two colonels exclaimed over and over again about the astounding ability of the Galloping Hogan and his Rapparees to avoid the large expanses settled by Williamite supporters and to circle around the ridges and high ground actually occupied by Williamite soldiers. The pattern became clear as we proceeded. Not once did we move on a ridge. The foothills of the three mountain ranges were always the backdrop. On the enemy side, rows of hedges would have blocked their view of the raiding party, which had to have moved by mounted pairs.

Colonel Hogan gave us a brief history lesson, explaining the concentration of Williamite supporters in the fertile valleys northeast, east, and southeast of Limerick City. Settlers from England and Scotland had been given the land after the Cromwell invasion, and many of the soldiers accepted land in lieu of the salaries owed them during their service. The area from O'Briens Bridge to Cappamore, with the point at Limerick City, made a pie-shaped plantation of Williamite supporters.

The Williamite supporters stayed to the east of the River Shannon; only rarely did a family settle on the west. The logic of the Galloping Hogan's route selection was becoming very clear, as we paused at Bridgetown to consider and discuss what was the single most critical part of the ride, the crossing of the River Shannon.

This would be the first time the 500 mounted troopers would leave the heavily wooded areas that had screened them. The most dangerous aspect was the Williamite guard on both sides of the Killaloe Bridge. Not only was the bridge denied the raiding party, but for some distance above the bridge there was relatively good visibility for the enemy guards. We took various positions at both ends of the bridge, and on some high ground on the west side. Then, simultaneously, we saw the solution as it had been seen by the Galloping Hogan. About 500 yards north of the Killaloe Bridge, a narrow spit of land jutted into the River Shannon from the east bank. We could see that if the Galloping Hogan went far enough north, keeping in the woods until the angle of the spit of land was favorable, the Shannon could be forded. The raiding party, shielded by the spit of land now known as Ballyvalley, then could continue east to the critically important rendezvous at Hogan's Glen. Colonel Hartigan made a major contribution at that point, for when we got to the approximate location of the ford, the Shannon was very wide and fast moving. Colonel Hartigan explained that the power plant erected along the banks of the Shannon had changed it from a deep channel to a sizable basin. I stood as close to the west bank of the Shannon as I dared, closed my eyes, and tried to envision the scene that night in

August 1690. Obviously, the first rider into the water would have been the Galloping Hogan, followed by Patrick Sarsfield, then his standard-bearer, junior officers, and then the troopers. Many of them would be taking their first deep breath of relief, as they realized they had survived the most important first crisis of the raid, the crossing of the River Shannon.

We reentered the car, and drove into Ballina, the first city in County Tipperary. Colonel Hogan, peering at his map of Sarsfield's Ride, alerted us with, "We're at Shallee, Hogan's Glen is not far ahead. Stop on this side of the Labbadiha Bridge."

Labbadiha Bridge had a substantial approach, but a small span over a chasm. We pulled the car off the road and walked to the span of the bridge. I looked down and saw—nothing. Nothing but thick foliage that obscured all but small patches of ground visible through the foliage. I felt let down, then realized what an idiotic reaction that was. Obviously, the Galloping Hogan would pick the least visible place for his head-quarters. I could hear the hum of water running, seemingly from a great distance. That made immediate sense—the Rapparees would need fresh water for themselves and their horses.

Since Ireland was in the grip of the wettest summer in history, I was well booted for my descent through the dense underbrush and sky-blocking branches and leaves. But I was not conditioned for the exertions. The rock-strewn path, through which water was running, was precipitous. I stumbled, slid, and levered myself down ten, twenty, thirty feet. The path didn't finally level off until at least fifty feet below the span of the bridge.

Now my perspective was utterly changed. The glen was more like the floor of a rain forest, completely obscured from view from above, with occasional rays of sunlight glancing through. There was more than a visual change. With each few feet of descent the noise of the water increased. I realized the sound was filtered or buffered, or both, by the successive layers of foliage above the stream. In the glen the sound was striking, the swollen stream rushed angrily by. Once again we were impressed by the skill of the Galloping Hogan in the selection of Hogan's Glen. No sounds, even neighing horses, could be heard on the bridge.

I turned from the clearing under the bridge and walked several hundred feet east, noting that narrow paths angled out in many directions like the spokes of a wheel with Hogan's Glen as the hub. It could be easily seen that hundreds of men and horses could filter into the glen from any point of a 180-degree semicircle and melt into the deep woods

in emergency. Several small streams emptied into the larger stream. I
bent down and picked what the Rapparees called *cress*, which we know
as watercress. Cress was another of the secrets of survival of the Rapparees. Somehow, they learned of its food value, and the typical meal
of an on-the-run Rapparee was a piece of dried or smoked meat, a dried
biscuit, cool fresh spring water, and a handful of cress.

I told Colonel Hogan and Colonel Hartigan about my discovery of
the cress and its source, another poem about the Galloping Hogan, parts
of which I had memorized. More or less verbatim I quoted it thus:

> As the cloud shadow skims o'er the meadow, when
> the fleet winged summer winds blow;
> By war-wasted castle and village and streamlet
> and crag doth he go;
> The foam flakes drop quick from his charger,
> yet never a bridle draws he;
> Till he baints [stops] in the hot blazing noontide
> by the cool fairywell of Lisbwee.
>
> He rubbed down his good charger fondly,
> the dry grass he reaped for its food;
> A crust for himself and a cress, with a
> drink of the sweet crystal flood.
> And he's up in the saddle flying
> o'er woodlands and broadfield once more
> Till the sand neath the hoofs of his charger
> is crunched by the wide Shannon's shore.

My two colonels were delighted, appreciative, and somewhat cha-
grined. They had never heard of the poem I had discovered. They asked
for more. I could only roughly remember the description of the Galloping
Hogan as he rode over the Irish countryside.

> You'd search from the grey rock of Cashel
> each side to the blue ocean's rim;
> Through green dale and hamlet and city,
> but ne'er find a horseman like him;
> With his foot as if grown in the stirrup,

his knee with its rooted hold ta'en,
With his seat in the saddle so graceful,
his sure hand so light on the rein.

We slid into our private thoughts, mine emotion-laden and somber. Then I thought I heard a sound. Or was it that I felt a presence? I turned to find the source, and saw a corridorlike break in the trees. As I looked, a ray of sunlight glanced down illuminating the stump of a great old tree. From a distance it looked like a plinth. Its position was such that I immediately *knew* that this was where the Galloping Hogan had stood to address his Rapparees. I decided then that I would return someday and erect a stone or wood sculpture of the Galloping Hogan on that natural plinth.

We rested there, at Hogan's Glen, as he and Sarsfield's band had, then resumed our journey, noting again that we never crossed a ridge, never lost our background on the far side, and always had a hedgeline on the near side. "This is Kiloscully," Colonel Hogan reported. "Ballyhourigan Wood is dead ahead." The second rest camp was in Ballyhourigan Wood, where more Rapparee reports were given to Sarsfield. It became evident that the artillery train commander's only choice was the area around the Ballyneety Castle ruins.

Colonel Hogan and Colonel Hartigan could also understand why. The area was hilly and the hedges high. The meadows, where they existed, were soft and marshy. The artillery pieces were huge, and would sink immediately once off the road, except in the cleared area around Ballyneety Castle.

We could envision the tension gripping Sarsfield and the Galloping Hogan at this point, but the tension melted and the battle fever grew as the report came in at dusk that the advance party of the artillery train had reached the Ballyneety area and was obviously preparing for the artillery to arrive within hours.

Again under cover, we left Ballyhourigan Wood and moved out of the foothills of the mountains toward Cullen, the village just four miles from Ballyneety. This was the first time in about ninety miles that Sarsfield's band was relatively in the open. But this area was Hogan territory. There were no Williamite farmers in this area, and Hogan's Rapparees sealed off the area and challenged anyone who moved. It was thus that the Williamite soldier's woman was found washing her tired and aching feet in the stream by which we stopped. We stopped also at the ruins of the tavern to which the Rapparee took her for drinks, getting from her the password of the Williamite camp.

Then they were in Cullen, still a tiny village, less than an hour's horse ride from Ballyneety. The troop and the Rapparees were gathered for the final instructions. I could almost hear the whispered instructions of Sarsfield: "No noise, lads, hand signals only. We'll advance by twos in column. The Galloping Hogan will get us into the camp without warning. When we hit the camp, sabers first, pistols only if they run, muskets last."

And I could almost hear the Galloping Hogan say to the Rapparees, "Run the horses directly back to Limerick City. There will be no need for secrecy. You, Ned-of-the-Hill, organize a rear guard to slow the pursuit as much as you can, then melt into the forests. The English rage will be terrible. They will shoot or hang every able-bodied man they find in the area."

At this juncture Colonels Hogan and Hartigan and I had slowly driven about ninety miles, with stops at Bridgetown and on the west bank of the Shannon, at Hogan's Glen and Ballyhourigan Wood. It had taken us less than five hours, driving very slowly and with frequent stops, to cover the distance ridden over by the Galloping Hogan and Sarsfield's band in twenty or more hours.

We drove the last four miles very slowly, each with his private thoughts. Then, suddenly, we were past the hedges and looking at the huge rock which towered above the only cleared area within miles, the fields around the old Ballyneety Castle. The conical-shaped mass is now known as Sarsfield's Rock. It had a magnetic attraction for us. We left the car and trudged through the boulder-strewn field, virtually unaltered for three hundred years. All meadowland in Ireland is grazing land. The cattle had kept the grass in check, and the huge stones of the old castle, lying where they had been thrown by the blast, stood out like sentinels. At the top of Sarsfield's Rock are two large marble plaques, beautifully carved in the old mode, with the story of Sarsfield's victory.

It was an extraordinary achievement—to what end?

7 ❧ The Treaty of Limerick

. . . three days later King William decided to raise the siege. It was his first defeat of this campaign.

HENRI AND BARBARA VAN DER ZEE,
William and Mary

SARSFIELD'S RIDE had many effects:

It restored the pride of the Irish, which was in tatters after the defeat at the Battle of the Boyne.

It alarmed King William, who returned to his near-hysterical wife, Queen Mary, who was harassed by yapping factions on all sides. He left the Baron de Ginkle in hopes that he would reduce Limerick to ruins and end the Irish War.

It gave to the ravaged, oppressed Irish heroes to sing about and talk about while they bore the rape and theft of their lands and churches and were denied the right to speak their language.

It gave Sarsfield time and bargaining room.

It saved the lives of thousands of officers and men who would have been killed, maimed or imprisoned if they had not chosen exile instead.

After many decades the Wild Geese and their descendants gained power and influence in France, Spain, Portugal, Italy, and Latin America, and they gave some strength back to Catholic Ireland, which gained its freedom in 1922. But it must be emphasized that the freedom of

74

Ireland was won *in* Ireland, by Irish men who fought, bled, and died there.

Not far from Limerick City, road signs now point to the route of Sarsfield's Ride. Its destination is Sarsfield's Rock, where the action took place. On foot, by cart and car, Irish men, women, and children and visitors can replicate the ride of Sarsfield and his troopers who, led by the Galloping Hogan, rode through a black night and part of the next day in mortal danger every mile of the way. If the ride to Ballyneety had not taken place or had failed, Patrick Sarsfield would not have survived as the sole romantic figure of the official army of King James II. If Sarsfield had not survived as a hero, the Galloping Hogan would have died forever with him.

Sarsfield and Hogan did succeed, however. Sarsfield then led the defense of Limerick with sufficient skill to achieve the Treaty of Limerick, an astoundingly mild and beneficial treaty for the native Irish. Two hundred and eighty-four years later, Sarsfield's Ride, as celebrated by the "Ballad of the Galloping Hogan," set me on this quest.

The success of the efforts of Patrick Sarsfield and the Galloping Hogan at Ballyneety, plus the pressure on King William to save Belgium from the French, led to the Treaty of Limerick, an astonishing victory for the Irish after a long and bitter military defeat.

This rueful poem, so mindful of the cliché about America never losing a war, never winning a peace, told it from the English point of view.

> Hard fate that still attends our Irish war,
> The conquerors lose, the conquered gainers are;
> Their pens the symbols of our swords' defeat,
> We fight like heroes, but like fools we treat.

The Treaty of Limerick is astounding and illuminating in several ways, so much so that certain paragraphs are shown here verbatim:

I. The Roman Catholics of this Kingdom shall enjoy such Privileges in the Exercise of their Religion as are consistent with the Laws of Ireland; or as they did enjoy in the Reign of King Charles the II: And their Majesties, as soon as their Affairs will permit them to Summon a Parliament in this Kingdom, will endeavour to procure the said Roman Catholics such further Security in that particular, as may preserve them from any Disturbance, upon the Account of their said Religion.

V. That all and singular, the said persons comprized in the 2d and 3d

Articles, shall have a general Pardon of all Attainders, Outlawries, Treasons, Misprisions of Treason, Premunires, Felonies, Trespasses, and other Crimes and Misdemeanors whatsoever, by them, or any of them committed since the beginning of the Reign of King James the II: and if any of them are Attainted by Parliament, the Lords Justices, and General, will use their best Endeavours to get the same repealed by parliament, and the Outlawries to be reversed Gratis, all but Writing-Clerks' Fees.

VI. And whereas these present Wars have drawn on great Violences on both parts, and that if leave were given to the bringing of all sorts of private Actions, the Animosities would probably continue, that have been too long on Foot, and the publick Disturbances last: For the Quieting and Settling therefore of this Kingdom, and avoiding those Inconveniences which would be the necessary consequences of the contrary, no person or persons whatsoever, comprized in the foregoing Articles, shall be Sued, Molested, or Impleaded at the Suit of any Party or Parties whatsoever, by them seized or taken, during the time of the War. And no Person or Persons whatsoever, in the Second or Third Articles comprized, shall be Sued, Impleaded or made accountable for the Rents or mean Rates of any Lands, Tenements, or Houses by him or them received or enjoyed in this Kingdom, since the beginning of the present War, to the day of the Date hereof, nor for any Waste or Trespass by him or them committed in any such Lands, Tenements, or Houses: And it is also agreed, that this Article shall be mutual, and reciprocal, on both sides.

Out of the careful reading of the Articles of Limerick and consideration of the mental attitudes of the native Irish came several significant circumstances, as follows:

The difference between the chivalry and tolerance of the English representatives at Limerick and Oliver Cromwell, the disciple of frightfulness in 1649 (just 42 years earlier).

The presence of Protestant English leaders who were willing to give religious freedom to the native Irish.

The pardon of all who fought with King James.

The arrogance, stupidity, and brutality of some of the English leaders led to the abrogation of the Treaty of Limerick in 1709. The English parliament passed what was known as the Popery Act, among whose onerous and unacceptable provisions were the denial of the right of native Irish to inherit land and the demand of an oath of allegiance to the Protestant Queen, Anne. This proved an absolute impossibility to most.

This treaty abrogation was to bring on over 200 more years of death, destruction, poverty, and misery to southern Ireland. The reasonableness and literacy of the language of the Treaty of Limerick, the benign provisions regarding religious freedom, and renouncement of repressions and retribution stand forth either as a beacon of statesmanship or as a deliberate doublecross to stop the Irish war at any cost, at least until the war with the French was over.

In any case, the breaking of the Treaty of Limerick by England had tragic results for both Ireland and England. It is somewhat astonishing to ponder that the English colonial empire started with tiny Ireland. And Ireland contributed to the destruction of the British Empire, at first indirectly through the Irish emigration to America where they made enormous contributions to the Revolutionary Army.

Two regiments of Irish troops came to the American colonies with the army of French General Rochambeau in 1780. In the mode of the times, these regiments were known by the names of the colonels commanding, Dillon and Walsh. They left France on March 27th, reaching Martinique six weeks later. From Martinique, French Admiral d'Estaing led them in the successful attack on the British island of Grenada. On the night of September 9th a small scouting party went ashore at Savannah, and the entire party landed in Georgia within the next few days.

As I left for France I had a sudden thought about the tragedy of Ireland being forty miles off the coast of England rather than the same distance off the coast of France or Portugal.

8 ❧ The Quest in France

PARIS EXCITED me the first time I saw it—in 1944 during World War II when I came back from combat in Aachen in Germany on a weekend pass. A half-dozen subsequent visits confirmed my belief that it is the most totally beautiful city in the world.

But this time, in January 1977, Paris-with-a-purpose lifted the trip to new levels of excitement. My first call, once settled at the Travellers Club on the Champs-Elysées, was to Le Comte Patrick de MacMahon, my benefactor extraordinaire in Paris. This estimable gentleman, on just the request of the Baron Pierre de Neufville, had made the long trip to Vincennes on the outskirts of Paris and persuaded the librarian to dig out the documents relating to Captain Jean Hogan and provide me with copies.

A lady, very French, answered my call. She switched to halting but well-articulated English when I spoke. "Ah, yes," she said, "Pierre said you . . . would be coming to Paris. Patrick . . . will be home at . . . seven. Please to call then. Merci." This lady was the countess, a smashingly attractive, tall, slender brunette whom I met the next evening.

When I did reach Patrick that evening, he was warm and most hospitable. "Can you join us for dinner tomorrow?" I assured him that I could. "Bien, we will expect you at seven. Number seventeen, rue Margueritte. Bien."

Rue Margueritte is one of the most stately and beautiful streets in Paris. Great five-story town houses line both sides, though few remain in use by one family. The MacMahons had half a floor, quite adequate for their four enchanting daughters, ages six months to eight years. Patrick was tall, much taller than the average Frenchman. He was dark and slender, but athletic looking. I noted immediately the aquiline Irish nose.

He introduced the countess as Trixie. He was in his mid to late thirties. I guessed Trixie was in her late twenties, looking far too young to have four children.

After dinner, he graciously brought the conversation around to the Galloping Hogan, asking if the documents he had gotten were useful. I extolled their virtues and brought out the English translations, laying them down one by one, indicating and reading the underlined critical statements:

February 15, 1726	War Request Decision
Hogan, retired lieutenant in the 1st Brigade of the Regiment of Lee	*Represents that he has served for 36 years beginning in a regiment which one of his relatives led to France; that many of his relatives were killed in service, including among others three brothers;* that he is riddled with wounds which reopen from time to time, which occasions him expense and places him in continuing need of the King's grace; and that he begs that the allowance he has received for several years may be continued.

"See, Patrick," I said, "Captain Jean Hogan says, 'a regiment which one of his relatives led to France.' That *could* have been the Galloping Hogan." I read on. "Many of his relatives were killed in service, including . . . three brothers."

Patrick expressed certainty that the army military records would yield their names, ranks, and ages. The second document read:

To His Grace the Duke of Chartres
    Hogan, Lieutenant in the First Brigade of Lée, represents that he arrived in France in 1691 as an officer in a regiment, and although he never

quitted the service, *the disbandment of some Irish troops and the death of several of his relatives who were lieutenant colonels in the Regiment of Clare prevented his advancement. Besides these relatives three of his brothers serving as officers were killed in the King's service; he now has a cousin who is a lieutenant general in the army of the King of Portugal* in whose service he too could have found advancement if his loyalty to the King's service had not prevented.

I read aloud: "The death of several of his relatives [probably not brothers] who were lieutenant colonels in the Regiment of Clare." I could get their names, I thought.

I continued reading: "He now has a cousin who is a lieutenant general in the army of the King of Portugal." "That could have been the Galloping Hogan," I said.

The battle in which he was wounded and his wounds were then described:

Hogan, Retired Lieutenant of the Brigade of Lée:
    M. de Lée, Lieutenant General, M. Mareschal, the King's first surgeon, and Mr. Dicconson, treasurer of the late Queen of England, have attested to his services, his wounds and his needs, and that he is burdened with a family.
    We the King's first surgeon attest that we were visited by Mr. Hogan, retired Lieutenant of the First Brigade of Lée. He has been wounded in the right leg, which was pierced through and through, and also received a wound in the left upper arm which broke his arm, as has several other wounds, one in the head, one in the hand, one in the neck and one in the left groin which went through his hip. He is in need of aid to take the waters. Done at Versailles in this 2nd day of March 1727. Signed, Mareschal.

"The poor devil was really shot up," I said.

"Those wounds," said Patrick, "sound as though he was hit by what they call grape, small metal pieces shot at close range from cannons."

"Ugh," I said. "That must have been hell. Without anesthetics or antibiotics, how did any of them live?"

"Apparently, the only cure was the waters, the mineral baths, to drain the wounds when they reopened," Patrick commented.

I put the papers away, then tried, without being too effusive, to tell Patrick what his help had meant to me. He made little of it verbally, but I could see he and Trixie were touched by my sincere expressions of gratitude and friendship.

My final night with Patrick and Trixie was unique and memorable. Another couple joined us. He was also a count, and his estates were contiguous with those of the MacMahons in Normandy. With almost childish glee, Patrick uncovered a record that contained the hunting calls of all the families in that area, the audio codes of the direction of their individual hunts.

For almost an hour Patrick played this record, which conjured up for me the vision of the MacMahons and their guests riding after the stag on horseback, a recreation still pursued. And all of this while we drank from several bottles of superb wine which bore the label LE DUC DE MAGENTA. The wine was from the MacMahon vineyards.

I walked alone for miles that night, partly to clear my head. I knew how a manic-depressive must feel most of the time. My success in Ireland and France was dizzying, considering my amateur status, and the degree of difficulty, and the nearly 300 years which had elapsed since the Galloping Hogan led the raid to Ballyneety. But now Portugal beckoned menacingly. What irony if the four Hogans there died ignominiously, and all records about them had been purged—a great way for a pilgrimage to end.

9 ❧ Portugal –
The Inquisition

I, Dom João [King John V of Portugal], advise
that having considered the merit and virtues of
Hogan, . . . I hope that he will serve me in
according to the reliance I place on him.

EL REY,
May 5, 1708,
Lisbon, Portugal

THE MORNING of January 25 I knew with certainty that I should go *immediately* to Portugal. Air France had a flight going to Lisbon, but the ticket seller, a sour-faced French girl, would not book a return flight to Paris. *"Le Strike,"* she said.

"L'autre airlines?" I asked.

"Oui, TAP and Varig."

But I took the plunge, knowing that it could be a mess if I were stranded in Portugal. Portuguese is a far more difficult language for me than was French, and it is *not* like Spanish.

I headed directly to the American embassy in Lisbon, where two young ladies at the U.S. Information Agency gave me the required application to the Nacional Biblioteca on Campo Grande ("Main Street") outside Lisbon, adjacent to the university. I didn't tell the girls more than the absolute minimum: "Writer working on a book and motion picture about the late seventeenth century."

Not a word about the Portuguese Inquisition, which was still an embarrassment to the mild, peaceful, tolerant Portuguese. My instincts nudged me away from any contact with officialdom at the Nacional Biblioteca, and I simply entered with the mob of students and others, asked for the card index file, and got the number of *Um Inquerido,* the book to which I had been referred by the military aide in the Portuguese embassy in Washington.

I got the number, wrote it large on the *requisio,* making a sloppy job of the book title, and received unsuspicious directions to the room where I could pick up my book.

I cooled my heels in the waiting room, had a few uneasy quarter hours awaiting my book, particularly when others, arriving later, got theirs while I sat. But then, not quite an hour after my entrance, my book arrived.

One look and I realized what a very difficult chore I had. Not reading Portuguese, I faced the scanning of every word for my key clues, "Hogan" and "Moura," the location of Hogan's command. The first thrill came when I spotted Moura, third on a list of cavalry regiments. But no list of personnel was included.

Disappointed, I looked around. To my left was a very, very old man with astonishingly young eyes. We nodded and smiled. To my right was an extremely lovely, sandy-haired young woman, who acknowledged my double take with humor.

I whispered, "Do you speak English?"

"Yes, I study English."

"Could you help me until your books come?" I asked.

"How could I help?"

"Just tell me what the introduction of this book says. When I know what the author intended, maybe I can figure out what chapters to concentrate on."

"I'll write it," she sighed. "Our neighbors might not appreciate the noise."

She wrote steadily for almost fifteen minutes. Her eyebrows lifted, her mouth pursed, when she realized the subject matter.

When the librarian approached with her book, I considered giving her a hip block or inviting her out for coffee, but knew neither would serve my ultimate purpose.

My neighbor handed me the handwritten pages, covered on both sides with a combination of printing and writing such as I use. I realized she had done most of the introduction. Her translation reads (my italics):

The Saint Office Court, or Inquisition, was established by the Pope Gregorie IX (1227–1241) against the heresies.

It was introduced in Portugal in the Kingdom of the fanatic D. Jose III, in 1531; it was abolished by the Portuguese revolution of 1829; it is the best investigation source for the studious one who wishes to know the evolution of the penal right in Portugal. The conscientious criminalist who wishes to relate the history of criminology in our country will have to consult [more than] the Archives, where the pages of the well-known court get old. Over the Inquisition much has been written and consulted to obtain *the biography of many men to whom Inquisition reached.*

Nevertheless, it is very interesting,—to know well the court mechanism is necessary to study detailedly one of the simplest processes, which has been achieved immediately after the beginning.

This was followed by a description of Lisbon.

This Inquisition record was highly significant, for in the interrogation of Dionisio Hogan, arrested because he joined the Masons, the whole family history of the Hogans in Portugal unfurled, and the mystery of the name Michael was solved.

The description of Lisbon was fascinating, but except for the opening line, nothing about the Inquisition or Hogan appeared there. With a smothered oath, I started through the book page by page. Then I spotted, in the footnote on page 7, the name *Hogan.* On page 8, four Hogans were named: Dionisio, André Miguel, Jacó, and João. I restrained my elation, for the next step was critical—getting copies of the key pages. I looked over the book to see if there were any prohibitions against copying. I could see none, but not understanding the language I was not filled with confidence. My hopes were not buoyed, additionally, by my understanding of the displeasure with which the Portuguese might view any publicity of that mark on their country's history.

I selected the single most important page for copying, sidled up to the young man who was very busy, and casually asked him for a copy of that page. He accommodated me without a glance at the contents of the page, which read:

Dennis (or Dionysius) Hogan, 30 years old, Irish, native of *Vilanova* county of Tipperary, lieutenant of cavalry in the *Alcantara* regiment, resident of *Janelas Verdes* (Green Windows), parish of *Santos.*[4] This Dennis Hogan came to Portugal in 1724 and was appointed cavalry lieutenant

---

[4] According to Father Charles O'Kelly, Hogan lived next to the Church of the Afflictions; according to *Mauricio Luis Magno,* he lived in the Rua das Flôres in the High Ward (or District).

on November 15, 1734, in recognition of services rendered to our country during nine years, by his uncle John Hogan; by letters-patent of January 25, 1754, Dennis Hogan was named *sargento-mór* of the cavalry regiment of the fortress of Moura. In the 18th century, the surname Hogan appears in various official documents of the Portuguese army, the following individuals all being related to each other: André Michael Hogan, *sargento-mór de batalha,* * father of Dennis Hogan; John Hogan, *sargento-mór de batalha,* brother of André Michael and uncle of Dennis; Jacó [Jacob?] Hogan, cavalry adjutant, a relative of the aforementioned. Dennis Hogan became a Mason in 1737.

I took the book to the copy room again and got copies of more pages. No problem, so back again for seven more.

I asked if I could leave for lunch without having the book returned to the archives. That was acceptable, the librarian said. She would hold it for me.

I put the twelve pages I had copied into the rented car, and returned after lunch. Two more visits to the copy room, and I had the entire section. Possibly my precautions against having too large a section of the book copied at once were needless, but I preferred to err on the side of overcaution and make sure I did get what I wanted. I did.

The Air France strike caused a run on seats on TAP (Portuguese Airlines) and Varig, making it necessary to stay in Lisbon one extra day. When I told my interpreter about Hogan and speculated about descendants, she said, "There are Hogans in Lisbon. One is João Hogan, our best modern painter. The other is Hogan Teves, a television newscaster."

I flew to the telephone and called the television station. "Señor Hogan Teves is not here now. He no longer broadcasts. He is now director of Public Relations."

I persuaded his secretary to give me his home number. He wasn't there yet but was expected. I noticed my breathing was shallow, an indication of my increasing stress. I relaxed and left my number and went back to concentrating on my interpreter.

Hogan Teves did call. He was trilingual, with Portuguese, Spanish, and French. His English was as bad as my Portuguese, so in French we agreed to meet the next morning. He sounded as though he considered me a bit mad when I suggested breakfast.

I waited in the lobby, wondering if I could spot Hogan Teves. A tall,

* This was a general staff rank, introduced into the Portuguese army in 1660, and it evolved rapidly. Apparently, this officer was a general.

light-haired man came in, and I thought "could be." I started toward him but stopped when he addressed a knot of other light-haired people in German. Most full-blooded Portuguese are dark-haired and brown-eyed, but there are some honey-colored blondes.

Then I saw a handsome, very well-dressed man in a corduroy jacket, vest, sweater, and slacks enter. He spotted me, smiled, and came directly to me.

"You are Matthew."

"Yes, Hogan. I'm delighted to meet you."

Handshakes, smiles galore, we went down to the coffee shop, exchanging basic French. We showed each other drawings of our family trees.

I was delighted, but the best was to come. For his aging father (then 78) had been preparing a card index file of their antecedents. He had brought the deck of cards with him. I rudely dragged him to the desk of the Lisbon Sheraton Hotel and called for the assistant manager, whose name, eerily, was Moura.

"Do you have a copying machine?" I didn't wait for him to answer, but pushed the cards forward, and said, "I *must* have copies. I'm flying out in two hours."

"Nó problem," he said. "We have a machine in the office."

He extended his hand to my companion and said, "You're Hogan Teves. I watched you every evening."

It was no surprise—TV newsmen are the new royalists everywhere.

Hogan Teves and I waited less than a half hour for the copies. I began to comprehend that Hogan Teves's family had to be one of the outstanding families, creatively, in Portugal—no politicians, no great industrialists, but an admiral, one fine writer, one traditional painter (now dead), and the best modern painter in Portugal.

I needed at that point only the final evidence linking the modern Hogans and Hogan Teves to the Hogans of 1706–1724. It came in the form of an art catalog in which the following statement appeared.

HOMAGE TO THE MEMORY OF RICARDO HOGAN

Ricardo Hogan or, more accurately, Ricardo Possolo Hogan de Mendonca, was a Portuguese artist, born of Portuguese parents. The name Hogan, which has contributed so much to the supposition that he was a foreigner (or "half-national" i.e. half Portuguese) came to him on the maternal side via his ancestor, João Hogan, the Irish captain who was invited by the Portuguese government to serve in our army and distinguished himself here in the defense of Campo Maior (near the Spanish border, approximately 60–75 miles north of Moura). João Hogan remained here and married a Portuguese woman; it was from that union that the artist was descended.

Hogan Teves gave me a dozen programs, newspaper clippings about Ricardo Hogan, the outstanding traditional painter of the early 1900s, and João Hogan, now the leading modern painter in Portugal. His work is so good it is displayed in the Gulbenkian museums in Lisbon and Paris—while he lives!

My next stop was the official home of all the ancient records of Portugal, the Tombo. Nowhere did the arrogance and stupidity of those Americans who consider themselves superior to "foreigners" seem so gross as at the Arquivo Nacional da Torre do Tombo in Lisbon.

I witnessed a performance of such efficiency and thoroughness as would do credit to the best teams of IBM or NASA scientist-researchers. I had four names—André, João, Jacó, and Dionisio Hogan—and sparse references to their military units. Two hours later, I had references to dozens of documents confirming arrival dates, battles, citations, marriages, children, and grandchildren—despite my not knowing what was going on around me. Eyes lit up; faces smiled and laughed with discovery; voices rose in crescendo and bounced off the walls. Books piled up, and one sweet lady wrote the references for me. What could be photocopied was ordered, as were copies from microfilm of those books that were too fragile to be handled. All of this buzzed around me while I sat like a dummy, smiling at everybody who looked at me. I suffered acute embarrassment then, as I recalled feeling a bit superior to Portuguese cooks and waiters and barbers I had met in the United States. These were the descendants of some of the most daring, intelligent, and dedicated men and women of the human race—the Portuguese, who sailed to Africa, South America, the Mediterranean, and the Pacific, and preserved nautical instruments and maps and records during the Middle Ages at Sagres in the Algarve.

The first order of King João V concerning the Hogans was cryptic:

NACIONAL ARQUIVO DA TORRE DO TOMBO
(DOCUMENT I-A)

It is my pleasure to order two officers, Dumcinol and Hogan, from the

Army of Flanders to serve as Brigadiers of Infantry in my Armies, with remunerations the same in their entirety as those paid to foreigners in the latter, suitable to the same posts, and with those of Captain of the same Infantry, with those due to Colonels of the Portuguese Regiments, except for bonuses

Accordingly, (I) order the Counsel of War to proceed with their Patents for Brigadiers. May 4, 1708.

El Rey

What was not located at this center the librarians identified as being available at the Arquivo Historie Militaire in Santa Appolonia Station. I rushed there, armed with the names of a Captain Coudeino and Colonel Campos e Souse, billed as "speaking well the English." It was not necessary to ask for them. I presented the names of the four Hogans, waited less than a half hour, and was presented with their dossiers. I seldom in my life felt more of a sense of accomplishment and appreciation.

The irrepressible hospitality of the Portuguese surfaced again. A Major Leal, who spoke English very well, approached me and offered his help. Our whispered conversation was overheard by a retired cavalry colonel, wise in the torturous ways of research involving "extincto military units," who hobbled all the way across the room with a typical cavalryman's gait to engage Major Leal in an animated conversation with frequent gestures toward me, my pile of books, the library walls and their thousands of books, other floors, other buildings, Moura, the Algarve, all of Portugal, all of Europe, and ultimately all of the world.

I couldn't understand one out of ten words, but Major Leal understood all. In essence, the colonel said: all librarians were idiots; all the soldiers assigned to do legwork in the Arquivo Historie Militaire were morons; the system was designed by a drunken, blind, mute Spaniard; there was no coordination between the national archives, the Tombo (where I had been so impressed), and the army archives; however, he had persevered and learned to overcome the chaotic labyrinth.

I saw an opening and asked Major Leal if the colonel might know a student or young researcher who, under his command, could beat the system for me. The result was exponentially more than my fondest hopes. Colonel, whom I suspected was bored stiff in retirement, said he would do it himself, "if I didn't need it tomorrow."

This fit exquisitely with my plan to leave Lisbon for the village of Moura, where all the Hogans lived while on duty and married or socialized with the Portuguese ladies, with whom they had many children.

Finally, and only after the colonel left, a quiet little man who had kept his nose buried in his books timidly approached me. His ancestors were from Spain, with whom Portuguese relations were not dissimilar to those of the Irish and the English. He told me I would waste much time in Moura if I didn't know in advance where the birth, marriage, and death records were centralized. He told me that all such records, over-flowing the little church storage rooms, had been collected by the Cath-olic Church in several larger parishes. He said he thought the records of Moura would be gathered at the parish of Beja. He then drew a map for me of how to get to a Franciscan convent, "where the record of which parish records went where" was kept.

I thought: my God, no wonder Vasco da Gama and Magellan were such great discoverers—the Portuguese had the greatest instincts and organization in the ancient world. Translated from the old Portuguese, the military records I had just been given read:

HOGAN (A.)

Experienced officer in the wars of Flanders, he was appointed Brigadier of Infantry in the Portuguese Army by decree of May 4, 1708, and *sargento-mor* by letter patent of April 30, 1710.

His full name was André *Miguel,* and that he was the father of the next officer. [My emphasis—*André Miguel was Michael!*]

Decree of May 4, 1708:

Dom João [King John V of Portugal] let everyone know that having considered the merit and other virtues of HOGAN and for the experience he acquired in the wars of Flanders, from where I ordered him to come to perform duties for me, I hope that he will serve me according to the reliance I place upon him. In this manner and with pleasure I appoint him, by this letter, Brigadier of Infantry in which military post he will be as long as I need him there, and he will receive the full pay according to his military post. . . . He will enjoy all honours, privileges, liberties, exemptions and liberality that belong to him directly and that are reported on the ordinances I ordered to be done and want to be kept inviolably. Thus I order the Governor of the Army to invest him in this military post ordering him to swear to observance of his duties and then let him perform his duties; Corporals of the Army honour him as a Brigadier of Infantry, officers and soldiers have to obey his orders entirely as you must and are obliged to do because you are under my service. The full pay above mentioned will be given at that time.

This letter was given in Lisbon on the 5th of May. Manuel do Rego do Morais did it in the year 1708 of the birth of Our Lord Jesus Christ. João Pereira da Cunha Ferras ordered to write it.

El Rey

By letter patent of April 30, 1710, he was invested lieutenant general:

Lieutenant of Cavalry HOGAN (Dionisio)

Son of the precedent and nephew of the next, he came to perform his duties in Portugal in 1724, and was invested Lieutenant of Cavalry of the Regiment of the Court, considering the services his uncle, João Hogan, rendered for nine years.

August 29, 1725.

I, the King, let everyone know that having in consideration the petition of Dionisio Hogan, son of André Hogan, born to him in the kingdom of Ireland, that has been serving me in the Cavalry of the Court for more than fifteen months as a soldier . . . he won a favourable verdict in the Trial Court of the Kingdom where he asked for consideration for the services of his uncle, João Hogan, born also in Ireland and son of Brian Hogan, who served in the military post of Sargento Mor in the Province of Alentego as well as in the Court since 1712 until 1723, the year he died. As I bestow privileges upon my vassals according to their merit, he, with greater reason, might expect greater generosity from me. He is a foreigner that left his native country to serve me in imitation of his ancestors and asked me that in consideration for his uncle and because he is performing his duties . . . the grace to invest him in the post of Captain of Cavalry, the only way to live decently in the kingdom according to his person. I got all information I needed and decide to appoint him in the military post of Lieutenant of Cavalry . . . and he will receive . . . half pay because he has not the years of service required in these Regiments.

Manuel Duarte Carriao did this letter, Lisbon, August 14, 1726. João Pereira da Cunha ordered to write it.

El Rey

By letter patent of January 25, 1754, he was appointed *sargento-mor* of the Regiment of Cavalry of Moura (a town in the province of Alentejo near the Spanish border).

Adjutant of Cavalry HOGAN (Jacob)

He is relative of the antecedents. He was appointed Adjutant of the Regiment of Light Cavalry that was formed at Tras-os-Montes, by decree

of January 7, 1709, having as Colonel, Pedro Francisco de Sa Sarmento.
Dispatch of the War Council of January 7, 1709.

Dom. João, etc. [King John V of Portugal]

I let everyone know that in consideration and respect for the merit and
virtues of Jacob Hogan and for his services in the Province of Tras-os-
Montes . . . I invest him, by this letter, Adjutant of the Regiment of
Light Cavalry that was formed in the Province of Tras-os-Montes where
Francisco de Sa Sarmento is in the post of Colonel.

He will serve in that military post . . . and he will receive the full pay
of sixteen "reis" a month and a house . . . and he will enjoy all honours,
privileges, liberation, exemption, and liberality referred on the military
ordinances that I want to be kept invoilably [sic]. So that I order Count
of Sao João of my Council, Army Governor of the Province of Tras-os-
Montes to invest him in this military post asking him to swear the observance of his duties and afterwards let him serve and act. Colonels and
Sergeants of this Regiment have to acknowledge the rank of his post as
Adjutant and all Captains and soldiers must obey his orders and the full
pay mentioned above will be payed in time.

Lisbon, January 23

Manuel do Rego do Morais did it in the year of Our Lord Jesus Christ
1709. João Pereira da Cunha ordered to write it.

El Rey

The following documents are just notes telling us of John Hogan's
arrival in Lisbon in August 1713. The document respecting his nephew
Dionisio Hogan says that he served in Portugal from 1712 until 1723,
the year he died in the military post of major general in the army of
Alentejo.

Sergento Mor HOGAN (João)

Manuel Duarte Carriao did it in Lisbon on May 29, 1713. João Pereira
da Cunha ordered to write it.

El Rey

Dom João [King John V] let everyone that reads this document know
that having in consideration the petition of João HOGAN, Major General of the Army at Campo Maior [a small town in Alentejo Province]
that asked me permission to come to the Court on business, which I
granted, has his absence registered on his service record and has not been
receiving pay for the time he was in the Court. Now I order him be payed
full pay.

Lisbon, August 10, 1713. Manuel do Rego de Morais did it. João Pereira da Cunha ordered to write it.

Having names, military ranks, and locations of their commands, my pace of acquisition of the Hogans' documents doubled. Lieutenant general André Miguel (Michael) Hogan was promoted to major general and received honors, money grants, and a house for "his gallantry at Campo Maior." There were enough references to the battle of Campo Maior to send me rushing to Portuguese history.

The battle was the final one in the Peninsular War, which involved the French, Spanish, and Portuguese. General André Miguel was the hero of that battle, described in general terms, but with no finite details that I could find in the limited time I had left in Portugal.

With regret, I put the heroic story of Major André Miguel Hogan aside until I could reach Colonel Pat Hogan whom I was certain could find confirmation. My most pressing need was the Inquisition trial-record translation. For security reasons I got an interpreter from the American embassy. For a modest twenty-five dollars I acquired the translation of *Um Inquerido*. The knot of fear started dissolving soon after I began reading the trial records.

Only Captain Denis Hogan had been arrested. He was questioned repeatedly, and in each episode, depositions were taken of all the eight Irish officers who had been arrested for joining the Masonic Order. There apparently was no torture. The tone of the interrogations started turning benign when Denis Hogan proved to the court that he had refused to take the oath of the Masonic Order in its entirety. He and the others had stated that nothing in the Masonic oath would in any way affect their belief in the Catholic Church and their loyalty to the king of Portugal.

The suspicion and the ire of the Inquisition switched to a Scotsman named Gordon, who had brought the Masonic Order to Portugal and wisely left the country. No longer considered heretics or disloyal to the Portuguese king, the group of Irish officers was released without prejudice. Denis Hogan, son of Michael Hogan, grandson of Brian Hogan of Ardcrony, went on to achieve the highest rank in the army available to a foreigner. He became a major general in 1754.

Vastly relieved, I returned to Major General Michael Hogan, the hero of Campo Maior in the Peninsular War of 1712.

It took me less than an hour to learn that the most despised villain in eighteenth-century Portugal was the Marquis de Bey of Spain. He was called the "Scourge of Portugal." He had led ravaging armies into Portugal treating soldiers and civilians with savage cruelty. We can only surmise that the surprise attack on Portugal in 1712 was an attempt to grab as much territory and loot as possible before the Peninsular War was finally settled. In point of historical fact, the peace conference was in progress at Utrecht when the Marquis de Bey slashed into Portugal with the obvious intention of capturing Lisbon and King João V, if possible.

The sole barrier to Lisbon was the fortified area known as Campo Maior, defended at the time by a very small garrison. According to the Portuguese records the town was under the command of the Count de Riberia. We can assume that the count was resigned to fighting to the death, given the reputation of his opponent.

Word was sent to Major General André Miguel Hogan at Moura, the headquarters of the Portuguese cavalry. General Hogan mustered a force of "between 400 and 500 men" and led the mounted troop miles through the darkness, eluding the sieging Spanish army. The reinforced garrison, then close to 700 strong, administered a stinging defeat on the Spanish army the next day, September 27th.

Elated, brimming with enthusiasm, I put in a long distance call from Lisbon to Colonel Pat Hogan, telling him what I'd found. He was guardedly optimistic. He had a fuzzy memory, he said, of a description of the Peninsular War from the viewpoint of the French, or of the Irish brigades with the French army. He promised to go to the Military History Society of Ireland at Newman House, University College, Dublin.

His zeal is attested to by the following. My request arrived on a Friday. Colonel Hogan, unable to find a typist and faced with a book too thick for photocopying, dove into O'Callahan's *History of the Irish Brigades* and copied the account of Major General André Miguel Hogan's heroic feats in longhand, as follows:

History of the Irish Brigades in the Service of France
John Cornelius O'Callahan (page 228)
The last affair of arms in this war between Spain and Portugal occurred in the campaign of 1712, under circumstances so creditable to an Irish officer as to deserve notice here, though that gentleman was not of the Irish Brigade. Notwithstanding the negotiations for peace at Utrecht, no truce having taken place by September between the two penisular kingdoms, the Marquis de Bey (styled "The Scourge of the Portuguese") appeared on the 28th, with nearly 20,000 men before Campo Maior in Portugal, and broke ground, October 4th–5th, the place being then in

anything but a condition to make suitable resistance. As, however, it was of the utmost consequence to preserve it, the Count de Riberia and a gallant French Protestant engineer officer, Brigadier de Massi, contrived a day or two after to make their way into the town with 200 or 300 Portuguese grenadiers, and *400 or 500 more Portuguese subsequently succeeded in doing so likewise, under an Irish officer, Major General Hogan— apparently the same "M. Hogan, Irlandoise,"* [my emphasis] Lieutenant Colonel in the Bavarian Guards, tried by Court Martial in 1706 at Mons for killing a Captain and countryman of his own in a duel, and hence, most probably, obliged to enter another service. Having assumed command of the garrison, the Major General took due measures for the defense. After battering and bombing the place from October 4th with 33 cannons or mortars, the Marquis de Bey ordered a grand assault to be made on the 27th, in the morning, by 15 battalions, 32 companies of grenadiers and a regiment of dismounted dragoons, under Lieutenant General Zuniga.

"By the help of a prodigious fire from their cannon and small arms," observes my English narrative of the *Compleat History of Europe*, for 1712, with respect to the enemy, "they made a descent into a part of the ditch that was dry and gave 3 assaults with a great deal of fury; but they were as bravely repulsed by the Portuguese under Major General Hogan, and forced to retire after an obstinate fight that lasted 2 hours, though the breach was very practicable, and so wide that 30 men might stand abreast in it. Their disorder was so great that they left most of their arms and 6 ladders behind. This action cost them 700 men killed and wounded, whereas the Portuguese loss did not amount to above 100 killed and 187 wounded; and such was their ardour that they pursued the enemy into their very trenches without any manner of order (notwithstanding the endeavours of Major General Hogan to put a stop to them), which might have proved very fatal to them, if the enemy had had courage to improve the opportunity."

The Spaniards next day raised this siege, stated altogether to have cost them 3,000 killed and wounded, to only about 400 Portuguese; a cessation of hostilities took place a few days after; and for such an honourable conclusion of this war was Portugal indebted to the gallantry of a Hogan, as, a century after, for the successful termination of a greater contest, to the discipline of a Beresford and the generalship of a Wellington.

This heroic performance of Major General Michael Hogan weighed heavily on the scale on which I endeavored to determine the true identity of the Galloping Hogan. I reread it several times, thrilled by it. Then suddenly it hit me like a physical blow—the astounding parallel of the night ride of the Galloping Hogan in 1691 in Ireland and the ride of General Michael Hogan in 1712 in Portugal. Both rides were through besieging enemy armies and resulted in resounding victories. About the same number of men and horses were involved.

I shook slightly from what amounted almost to adrenaline shock. When I settled down I realized two profound facts. First, I was then absolutely convinced that Major General André Miguel Hogan, hero of Campo Maior, General Michael Hogan of the army of Louis XIV, Michael Hogan of Doon and Ardcrony, and the Galloping Hogan were one and the same. And second, my objectivity was gone and I needed a judge and jury to act as devil's advocate.

Forewarned about the accursed vice of the Irish, the spirit of rivalry and jealousy, I knew what cynicism and ridicule could await me in Ireland. I needed time to think. What better place than the Eternal City, the Vatican in Rome? I booked a flight to Rome, but only after hosting a marvelous dinner in one of the many superb restaurants in Lisbon for Major Leal, the two beautiful girls from the American embassy, and the retired cavalry colonel who had helped me so much.

Late that night I vowed to tell anyone who would listen about the wonderful people of Portugal, among the least appreciated, most civilized race in the world. Their colonial policies were such that they left effective infrastructures in all the countries they explored and assumed responsibility for. They were truly "color blind," and many Portuguese who settled in various countries married into races of many hues, with excellent effect.

For all past centuries they welcomed people from other lands, many of them oppressed. They welcomed the Hogans in 1706 and thereafter, and John Hogan, brother of Michael, started a line of Irish Portuguese which has brought honor to each race.

I left Portugal with the warmest possible feelings about the country and the people. I hoped to find Rome relatively as hospitable. It was a vain hope.

10 🍀 The Runaround in Rome

Gentlemen . . . how many religious, blue-eyed, red-faced, red-haired Italians have you met in your life?

JUDGE WILLIAM HUGHES MULLIGAN,
speech before the Friendly Sons of Saint Patrick,
New York City

THE TRIP to Rome started pleasantly enough, with several drinks and a good-natured flirtation with a smashing Alitalia stewardess. During the flight I dove into the packet of material I had assembled on Rome and the Hogans, including the report that a Donal Hogan, who had been a simple priest in Ireland, had been made the bishop of Tesula in the seventh century.

One of my good friends had given me a copy of the speech made by Judge William Hughes Mulligan at a Saint Patrick's Day celebration in New York. I got such a treat and laughed so often and loud that the stewardesses and my fellow passengers must have concluded that I was quite mad. My only concern was that the Italian customs officials would deny me entry into their placid country or clap me in jail for bringing such dangerous and inflammatory material into Italy.

Judge William Hughes Mulligan said, in part:

> I am honored indeed to be in such distinguished company and to be invited to respond to the toast "The Day We Celebrate."
>
> Toasting reminds me of an Irish friend who, when asked that most welcome question, "Will you have another drink?" responded, "I only

answered that question in the negative once—and that time I misunderstood the question."

I thought it might be appropriate, on this evening particularly, to comment on some Irish achievements and characteristics not generally appreciated or in fact even known.

A few years ago when I was in Ireland, I visited the ancient port city of Galway where I was assured by a local that Christopher Columbus had stopped there to bring on board an Irish navigator, who actually guided him to the New World.

A few months ago I was in the company of the chief judge of the Supreme Court of Ireland, a typically urbane, scholarly, and intellectual Irishman, not given to the easy acceptance of leprechauns or unfounded legends. I asked him about the story of the Irish navigator, and I was frankly surprised when, instead of debunking it, he responded, "Oh yes, the story is well authenticated. The man's name was Lynch."

With all due respect, I could not accept the story; there was no record that Columbus ever made any such diversion to Galway, pleasant though it might be. It seemed much more logical to me that Lynch, great sailor that he must have been, had sailed from Ireland to Spain and was the navigator from the start.

Becoming more interested, I studied the celebrated work on the subject, Samuel Eliot Morison's *Admiral of the Ocean Sea,* and I discovered to my dismay that Lynch's name does not appear on the list of the crew of any of the three vessels. This in turn led me to a somewhat spectacular discovery which I must share with you tonight in the privacy of this room. Morison's book gives a physical description of Columbus, which was provided by his own contemporaries, including his son. At pages 40 to 41 I quote:

"He was more than middling tall, aquiline nose, blue eyes, complexion light and tending to bright red, beard and hair red. When he was angry he would exclaim, 'May God take you.' In matter of religion he was so strict that for fasting and saying all the canonical offices he might have been taken for a member of a religious order."

Gentlemen, in all honesty and frankness, how many religious, blue-eyed, red-faced, red-haired Italians have you met in your life?

Friendly Sons and friends, I am not only suggesting but I think the facts clearly establish that in reality Columbus was Lynch—or Lynch was Columbus—whichever way you want it. There is even further evidence— Morison, who claims that Columbus was born in Genoa, admits that Columbus could not read or write Italian—neither could Lynch. Morison—and we, of course, could expect no help from Samuel Eliot Morison—further states that Columbus spoke Spanish with a Portuguese accent. Actually, of course, it was Irish he spoke, and isn't it a mark of Lynch's great leadership and seamanship that he could make that Mediterranean crew understand his orders, even though they were given in Gaelic.

Gentlemen, we have convicted men of serious crimes in the Federal Court on less evidence than we have here—and my court affirmed them.

Of course, Mr. Vice-President, it is only logical and reasonable for us to assume that the great Irish seamen who visited Italy, and for all I know may have discovered it, undoubtedly took the Greek Island tour. We now know that it was their custom to adopt the names of the natives. My only regret is that my work on the Court has precluded me from establishing the true identity of Plato, Socrates and Aristotle. It is interesting, however, to note that Socrates died after drinking too much hemlock, which affords us some small indication that his origins were in some colder clime. . . .

Gentlemen, although few of us were born in Ireland, most of us were all reared in a distinctly Irish tradition—it was marked by a fierce devotion to our faith. It was a demanding faith of fast and sacrifice and self-discipline. The tougher it was to follow, the easier it was for the Irish to pass down to their children. Now that its strictures have been somewhat relaxed, it will be so much more difficult to give and bequeath or even to inherit. But we will meet the challenge. We also inherited from our Irish forebears a fierce love of country—in peace or in war. Particularly, perhaps, in war, we contributed much more than our share. But why shouldn't we love America? After all, we discovered it.

God bless you.

The Italian customs agents and police were so busy hiding from the Red Brigades that I did get into Rome, and to the Vatican, with my incontrovertible evidence that an Irishman named Lynch actually discovered America. But, I didn't press my luck by showing it around, though I was sufficiently irritated by the runaround I got at the Vatican that I was sorely tempted to post Judge Mulligan's speech on the Vatican bulletin board.

My first visit to the Vatican was very much like a visit to IT&T, where Pope Harold Geneen reigns supreme. Priests and bishops and cardinals scurried in and out, stone-faced, thin-lipped, with their black attaché cases and stress-ravaged faces.

Some relief was supplied by the many sweet-faced nuns coming and going across Saint Peter's Square. The old-fashioned black garb has yielded to the modern dress, with an understandable change in the personalities of the nuns. And, the hordes of the faithful, from many lands, were wide-eyed and respectful.

I had reason to expect a warm welcome at the Vatican archives. Four O'Hogans had been bishops. The Hogans had earned the reputation as an ecclesiastical family. And, on the Culligan side, a relative, Father Culligan, had been one of the leaders of the archeological operation that discovered the tomb of Saint Peter. So, I thought some cooperation was not unreasonable to expect.

I was wrong, for a reason I should have anticipated. The Roman Curia, which literally runs the Vatican, is almost entirely Italian— inbred and astoundingly bureaucratic. They exhibit an attitude of superiority that cannot be obscured by the frequent displays of humility.

I could not break through to the nominal head of the archives, so I settled for members of his staff. Each of them started each conversation by raising his eyes heavenward and turning the palms of both hands outward and upward, murmuring in Italian, "It is not possible."

In the one instance in which I seemed to be making progress, after I enumerated the bishops of the family and the exploits of Father Culligan, archeologist, I made the mistake of telling the priest that Father Edmund Hogan, S.J., had spent years in Rome, digging into the records about ancient Ireland. That finished me. He said, "Then there would appear to be little need of your repeating his efforts. Is it not so?"

I left the Vatican archives nursing my first defeat in the five years I had been researching the Clan Hogan. My anger melted rapidly when I learned from several sources that Paul VI was a very old, frail, and ailing pontiff at the time I was there. When the leader of any enterprise nears death, the bureaucracy reigns supreme. I realized that I had been rebuffed by the system, not consciously by any hostile individual. It was also to be expected that the Romans, many of them living off the Vatican in a bewildering range of activities, would recognize the viability of services to the thousands of scholars, students, writers, and researchers pouring into Rome at all seasons. So, over the decades the coterie of "approved" researchers in Rome has grown.

It is impossible for anyone to gain access to the Vatican archives unless officially approved and holding a card, confirming that approval. Then I got the message. Only a privileged few Romans are issued these cards, and anyone seeking information must employ one of them at a not-inconsiderable cost.

Fortunately a far better solution was provided for me by a combination of Colonel Pat Hogan and the late Father Edmund Hogan, S.J., cited by MacLysaght and eulogized by Professor Douglas Hyde.

With the intense dedication which characterized his help to me, Colonel Hogan spent hours searching in the National Library in Dublin for a series written by Father Hogan for the long defunct *Limerick Reporter*. He had noted a reference to "A History of the O'Hogans" among the more than eighty books written and/or edited by the good Father Hogan. Colonel Hogan finally found the series in the closing issues of 1872. Father Hogan had spent many years in Rome, without any restrictions, and, as an ecclesiastical family, the Hogans had been well chronicled at the Vatican.

He too had realized the need for outside corroboration of Irish family histories, and by cross-referencing O'Donovan and O'Curry, two renowned Irish historians and scholars, with the Vatican archives, he had pieced together his history of the O'Hogans that had appeared in the *Limerick Reporter*.

I felt that his report had to be taken seriously for these reasons:

He was a highly regarded scholar at this time of his life and would hardly jeopardize his standing with his peers with bogus family history.

He was a member in good standing of the Society of Jesus, the Jesuit order, and subject to the discipline of the order.

He was well aware of the skepticism of Irish scholars and critics about family histories.

His report was in a widely circulated newspaper in County Limerick that had a large readership in County Tipperary and County Clare.

The Vatican archives, to which he had free access, were (and are) highly regarded by scholars of all races and religions, being the oldest continuous administrative records in the Western World.

The opening lines of his report made me very, very sorry that I had not known Father Edmund Hogan. His waggish sense of humor shone through. Father Edmund Hogan's preamble, written for all Ireland to see, read:

> The Hogans are a modest and undistinguished clan. Their name should not be breathed; they should be let "sleep in the shade" and is it not a wanton piece of impertinence and pedantry to interfere with the modest obscurity which they enjoy?

Having gotten that off his ample chest, he wrote:

Each monarch of Erin had a learned Ollam attached to his court, whose office it was to keep a genealogical history of all the descending branches of the royal family and of the families of provincial kings and territorial chiefs, in order to decide conflicting claims by an impartial public record. Moreover each provincial king and territorial chief had his own Ollam, whose records, according to pre-Christian law, were compared every third year with the records of the Chief Ollam at Tara, and again every principal family kept its own pedigree . . . as every freeborn man was, according to law, entitled by blood to succeed to the chieftaincy, and to a legal share of the lands of the sept.

Hence the pedigrees, which were the only proofs of title to land and dignity in the clan, were kept with jealous care and accuracy; and hence also Ogaan O'Hogan, chief of his name in the sixteenth century, could, as well as the O'Briens, trace his descent through thirteen hundred years from Oilloll Olum, King of Munster, who died in AD 234, and whose reign falls within the authentic period of Irish history. (See O'Curry, O'Donovan pedigree of the O'Brien's in the *Battle of Magh-Rath*.) Of the accuracy of the O'Brien genealogy, Dr. O'Donovan says, there can be no reasonable doubt; and the same must be said of the O'Hogan's, which is identical with the former up to the reign of Brian Boriome.

My sparse results at the Vatican archives probably were partly responsible for my final thoughts each night before sleeping: tomorrow was the day Rome would not work. Political, economic problems, terrorism, the greed and indifference were evident everywhere, including the Vatican. But, somehow Rome did continue to function, and I felt I was functioning too, as soon as I started walking.

The one activity I had neglected in the preparation of this book, I realized, was quiet reflection, that wondrous meditation which converts news, information, comment, knowledge into understanding. There is a marvelous way to walk in Rome (as in Paris), crossing and recrossing the Tiber River on the many parallel bridges. With this technique, the walker can cover many miles, get what breeze is stirring in Rome, and never get very far from Saint Peter's Square. That was important to me, for that is where I rested after each few hours of walking.

I had my corner, on the right side of the square, which gave me an oblique view of this emotionally gripping monument to the world's greatest builders and artists. I think that anyone who spends time in Saint Peter's Square will very soon deliberately or involuntarily think about survival.

So, the survival of Ireland and the Irish, with their characteristics and qualities intact, became my primary holistic exercise. Arnold Toynbee arrested attention with the fine phrase, "challenge and response."

Ireland was cruelly challenged, for over a thousand years, and responded with rebellions every fifty years or so, which bled the country white. But it survived.

In the *Simpleton of the Unexpected Isles,* George Bernard Shaw's character PRA said, "Judgement is evaluation. Civilizations live by their valuations. If the valuations are false, the civilization perishes. . . . We are not being punished, we are being valued."

I thought, in Rome, that perhaps I had overemphasized hope as the force in the Irish psyche that made all things possible. Surely faith was the more active force. There are as many descriptions of faith as there are describers. My favorite is "the bird that feels the light and sings when the dawn is still dark." The dawn was dark in Ireland for over a thousand years, but the Irish felt the light, described by John Hay.

> For always in thine eyes, O Liberty
> Shines that high light whereby the world is saved
> And though thou slay us, we will trust in thee.

Then I knew that the trip to Rome had been providential. Rome had slowed me down, and new feelings were being given time to emerge from my individual subconscious.

I perceived then that the "high light" of Liberty had not penetrated some of the dark corners of Ireland and the Irish mind, body, and emotions. The Republic of Ireland had political liberty and growing economic liberty, but the residual bitterness, the thirst for revenge, and the recrimination were Ireland's present oppressors, now and for as long as decent, normal Irish men and women, both Catholic and Protestant, in the South and in the counties of the North, permitted it to be.

I left downtown Rome for the airport with a new internal calmness that one can experience after a religious retreat or prolonged meditation. My resolve to retain that calmness was tested almost immediately, when I reached the Rome airport. The baggage handlers went on strike; all planes were delayed; and I had already gone through customs. There was no information about flights, the attendants became less and less civil. But, instead of "burning," I sat calmly and tried to think of what one man could do to alleviate the acrimony and personal conflict in Ireland.

My wait at the Rome airport was eleven hours—the all-time record for me. Somewhere about the halfway point an idea surfaced that sparkled. One man could give millions of dollars to certain programs in

Ireland or devote years to managing them. I had nothing to give but ideas, perhaps one great idea. The concept that sparkled was the world's first international college of marketing as an adjunct to either Trinity College or the University of Dublin.

The rationale was simple. The young Irish boys and girls coming out of the equivalent to our high-school systems are among the best educated in Europe. The Irish have a genetic facility with language and a general charm and humor. These qualities are essential to the salesman and the marketing manager. The graduates of the international college of marketing would be the most sought after in the industrial democracies. Admissions would follow merit examinations that would be available to men and women, northern and southern, Catholic and Protestant, as well as to the youngsters of Irish-French ancestry, making the college a bilingual one.

Within a decade there would be hundreds, thousands, of Irish men and women in the great multinational corporations of the world, and Ireland would be spared the tragedy of further migration. They would be a modern version of the Wild Geese, but without the terrible result of "all that delirium of the brave" of the first flight, about which William Butler Yeats wrote:

> *Was it for this the wild geese spread*
> *The grey wing upon every tide;*
> *For this that all that blood was shed, . . .*

Too much Irish blood and Hogan blood has been shed in Ireland, France, Spain, Holland, and Portugal "in every cause but our own." But, God willing, never again.

My plane left for Ireland half a day late, and I arrived back in Dublin ready to take my case—that André Miguel Hogan, Michael Hogan of Doon, and the Galloping Hogan were one and the same man—to my devil's advocates, Father Henry and Colonel Pat Hogan.

11 ❧ FatheR HenRy –
The Deuil's
Aduocate

*You found what you were looking for, Matthew,
the spirit of the Irish. You may never know for
sure who the Galloping Hogan was. Does it really
matter anymore?*

FATHER HENRY

BECAUSE OF Father Henry, I had decided to learn more about the Capuchin Order. What I learned sent me loping back to his office for a kind of catharsis before I made my final evaluation of all the gathered evidence. The Capuchins are perhaps the most scholarly order as to temperament in the Catholic Church. They have been avid historians, writers, and editors. Father Henry was the ideal sounding board for concepts and ideas. And, just as my mother, Sarah Jane Hogan, was the most honest woman in my life, Father Henry was, I felt, the most honest man. He too, early in my search, had warned me about bogus Irish family histories and was aware—much more than I—of likely and unlikely pitfalls in a search such as mine.

I brought a bottle of Power's Irish Whiskey and the biggest Cuban cigar I could find. Father Henry, his face aglow, expanded in his role as judge and jury, as I made my case to prove that Michael Hogan of Ardcrony and Nenagh, County Tipperary, was the Galloping Hogan. I reviewed all the possibilities.

Was the Galloping Hogan killed by the vengeful pursuers under Villiers after the Ballyneety raid? The Percy poem had said a "blade is wet with Hogan's life-blood."

104

Father Henry: Impossible. The death of the Galloping Hogan during such an exploit would have spawned a dozen ballads in his honor. All the ballads and records state that he led Sarsfield back to Limerick.

Colonel Pat Hogan said he heard, as a boy, that Hogans *did* die in the Ballyneety raid that day.

Father Henry: It is very likely that one or more Hogans were in the rear guard. The Hogan's blood mentioned in the Percy French ballad probably referred to one of those Hogans.

Desmond Rush, of the *Irish Independent,* received three letters regarding the Galloping Hogan when he wrote about my search. One said he was executed by the British at the fort at Cashel. The second said he was killed in a battle with other Rapparees over amnesty from the British. The third said his name was Michael, and he was from the village of Doon, along the route of Sarsfield's Ride, but he deliberately dropped from sight after the ride. What is most likely?

Father Henry: One is unlikely for the reason I gave you for your first premise. If the British executed him there would have been records and ballads and songs by the dozen. Number Two is illogical, since the Treaty of Limerick gave a blanket pardon to *all* who fought with King James. There was no need for a battle regarding an amnesty which was already granted. Number Three is the most likely, particularly the dropping out of sight. The English must have thirsted for the blood of Hogan—reprisals were a common weapon of all occupying armies in those terrible days.

Desmond Rush also received a letter much more recently from a reader in Roscrea commenting on the report of the Protestant chaplain, Reverend Storey, that the Galloping Hogan was killed in a battle with other Rapparees near Roscrea. This reader fairly called attention to the hatred of the Reverend Storey because the Galloping Hogan had killed his son in a skirmish there. I went all the way to the British National Library to try to find some evidence. All I could find was the Reverend Storey's last will and testament, in which he gave everything to widows and orphans. He did not have a son, but there was an Ensign Storey, his nephew, who was killed in a skirmish with Rapparees led by the Galloping Hogan.

Father Henry: Well, you'd get good marks for trying. There might have been ill-will prompting some spirit of revenge if the Galloping Hogan did kill Ensign Storey, the chaplain's nephew.

I pored over literally hundreds of proclamations of Baron Ginkle, the head of King William's army. There were proclamations offering rewards of twenty guineas for the arrest or killing of some Rapparees, but not a single mention of Hogan did I find. That led me to the conclusion that the Galloping Hogan, brothers and cousins, went into the army of Patrick Sarsfield, and gained protection under the Treaty of Limerick.

Father Henry: Who can say otherwise with any certainty?

Your friend at the monastery rather apologetically startled me by asking if all three stories could be true. He asked if it were not possible that more than one member of the Hogan family used the identity of the Galloping Hogan to confuse the English.

Father Henry: Well, now, there is no question that the Rapparees did confuse the English. The Protestant chaplain, Storey, who traveled with the Williamite army, was also the historian of the Irish campaign. He wrote that there would be no sign of a single Rapparee during daylight hours, then four or five hundred would appear for a raid, carry out the mission, then melt into the bogs and woods, to reappear hours later for another raid. It is certainly possible.

The oldest man I could find in the Clan Hogan area said Hogan's Glen had been described to him by his father and grandfather. It was at Shallee, close to Doon, and along the route of Sarsfield's Ride. The official report of Sarsfield's Ride said that the Galloping Hogan led Sarsfield's band to Hogan's Glen, where they rendezvoused, and met Hogan's Rapparees.

Father Henry: Strong corroborating evidence, the pieces are fitting together.

The French army records state that one Hogan led a regiment out of Ireland with Sarsfield and Mahon. It was kept intact. Then the French *and* Portuguese and Irish records state that General M. Hogan killed a fellow Irish officer in a duel in Flanders and left France to join the army of King João V of Portugal. How would you evaluate that?

Father Henry: The Hogan who led a full unit of Irish troops out of Ireland and was confirmed as its leader by the French army command must have been a highly respected clan chieftain. We know Patrick Sarsfield became a general and, on his death, a marshal. Mahon became a general. Michael Hogan became a general. Were it not for the outlawed duel, he might well have become a marshal of France. There is no doubt, I think, that Michael Hogan had the ability and the leadership qualities to be the Galloping Hogan.

At this point, I read to Father Henry the accounts from the Portuguese and Irish history of Major General André Miguel Hogan's heroic defense of Campo Maior in Portugal in 1712. Then I presented my next premise.

There is an astounding parallel to the Galloping Hogan's guiding of Sarsfield's troops to Ballyneety and André Miguel Hogan leading his own troops through the Marquis de Bey's sieging army to the defense of Campo Maior. In fact, the number of men used is even the same. What would you make of the similarity?

Father Henry: Well, that would stretch coincidence much too far, that there would be *two* Hogans about the same age, with the same methods of operation, and the same kind of ability.

Captain Jean Hogan, in his supplications to the King of France, said that three of his brothers and three cousins, captains and colonels, were killed fighting in the Regiment of Lee and the Regiment of Clare. The Portuguese military records prove that Michael and two of his brothers, John (João) and Jacob (Jacó), survived the battles in France and joined Michael (André Miguel) in Portugal. João became a major general and Jacó an adjutant. The French, Portuguese, *and* Irish records state that they were the sons of Brian Hogan of Ardcrony; Doon is in Ardcrony.

Father Henry (with a chuckle): Men have been jailed, hanged, and shot on less evidence than you've assembled, Matthew. Obviously, as a priest, I can't swear to the good Lord that Michael Hogan was the Galloping Hogan, but I think you'd be justified in believing that he was.

"One last question, Father," I said, "If Michael Hogan was the Galloping Hogan, why did he drop that identity completely after Ballyneety?"

"We can only guess," he replied, "but consider the situation. Most of the old families were destroyed and their lands taken after 1540 by the army of Henry VIII when he broke with Rome and started the Church of England. The brutal Earl of Rosse led the attacks against the clans in Tipperary, Limerick, and Clare. The surviving men, women, and children fled into the wooded slopes and mountains. The Rapparees appeared and armed themselves by raiding their conquerors. They, their priests, and their families were hunted, hanged, tortured, and killed.

"You can imagine the hatred and thirst for revenge and reprisals on both sides. There were many, many Hogans in the area. Michael Hogan, deciding to leave with eight brothers and cousins, must have thought of two things—reprisals against his immediate family and the future usefulness of the legend of the Galloping Hogan as an inspiration. I would guess his decision, assuming Michael was the Galloping Hogan, was compounded of at least those two parts."

My next step was to visit Colonel Pat Hogan for his evaluation.

The gradual change in Colonel Hogan's attitude about the ancient Clan Hogan was a continuing, marvelous stimulant for me. At first he had actually said, "Except for the Galloping Hogan, I always thought they were probably horse holders for the better known chiefs." His interest and pride expanded greatly when I sent him the tribute to Edmund Hogan by Douglas Hyde, the great Irish scholar and President of Ireland from 1938 to 1945.

The warmly evocative portions of the tribute, in the magazine *Studies*, read:

CHRONICLE.

I.—A Great Irish Scholar
BY PROFESSOR DOUGLAS HYDE, LL.D., D.LITT.

At a ripe old age, loved and admired by a large circle of friends, and honoured by scholars in many countries, there passed away from us, on the 26th of November, the Rev. Edmund Hogan, S.J., D.Litt. A connecting link with the era of O'Donovan and O'Curry, he was himself a distinguished and brilliant scholar, a pioneer in many fields of Irish history, philology, and topography.

Dr. Hogan was born on the 23rd of January, 1831, near the Cove of Cork. He entered the Jesuit Order at the early age of sixteen, and was ordained nine years later. The amount of active professional work which he accomplished was enormous, and would have certainly undermined any but the most robust constitution. He worked both on the Continent and at home. He was one of the founders of the Sacred Heart College in Limerick, and he remained there from 1859 to 1865. From thence he proceeded to Rome, and while in the Eternal City he ransacked the Roman Archives, especially those relating to Ireland, and acquired a vast mass of information about the bygone history of his own Order in its relation to the Irish nation. One of his earliest books, published as far back as 1878, was the edition of a hitherto unpublished MS. entitled "Description of Ireland and the state thereof as it is at this present in Anno 1598." The text of this, in itself a rather brief description of the Irish counties and the principal families inhabiting them, he used as a vehicle for conveying an astounding amount of information of his own— geographical, historical and genealogical.

He was already engaged in 1900 upon what may, I think, be his magnum opus, the book by which more than any other he will always be remembered, his *Onomasticon*. This vast compilation, containing 700 double pages of close print, has been the object of his study for ten years. It is a book which is, and will remain, indispensable to every student of Irish literature. . . .

Though his family spoke Irish, yet Dr. Hogan was not brought up as an Irish speaker. I think it was the reproach of some foreign priest, who rebuked him for not knowing his own language, which first turned his thoughts to the study of its treasures. He also knew many foreign tongues, and corresponded with friends and scholars in many countries. He had a fine presence, his head was handsome, his forehead broad, his eyes kindly, and his manner always courteous and agreeable. There was about him a kind of massive dignity and an impressive imperturbability of temperament. With all his great learning he was charmingly simple, and delighted in anecdotes about people whom he had met and known. One could scarcely mention an Irish family about whose past he had not much to tell. He had a regular passion for genealogy, which combined with his phenomenal memory would have made him an ideal editor of Mac Firbis's or O'Clery's works on this subject. His room used to be littered—shelves, tables and floor—with books, journals, papers and rare volumes, beyond any room that I have ever seen—and yet he always found what he wanted. His whole life was indeed dedicated "dochum glóire Dé agus onóra na h-Eireann" [to the glory of God and the honor of Ireland].

After reading that tribute to Father Hogan and considering its author's credibility, Colonel Pat Hogan became an avid ally, contributing mightily to both my quest for the Galloping Hogan and the spirit of the Irish. His greeting and his reaction to my request that he also play devil's advocate delighted me.

I presented my argument to Colonel Hogan in much the same manner as I had to Father Henry. Colonel Hogan was struck, as I had been, by the breathtaking parallel of the Galloping Hogan's night ride to Ballyneety in 1690 and General André Miguel Hogan's ride to Campo Maior in 1712. He now felt, as did Father Henry, that *I* was justified in concluding that they were one and the same man, though, of course, he could not be certain.

The Portuguese records do not show the details of the further service of Major General André Miguel Hogan, or of his death and burial place. Major General João Hogan was killed in battle in 1723. The activities of Adjutant Jacó Hogan are unrecorded. The full career of Dionisio Hogan is thoroughly documented. He rose to major general in 1757.

Sometime before 1800, members of the Wild Geese of Ireland became ministers, diplomats, doctors, architects, lawyers, priests; writers, painters, and sculptors. Some went into a wide range of other activities—shipping, building, trading. Thousands went to America, many becoming government officials.

When the American Revolution came, over a quarter of the army were Irishmen. Thirty-six general officers were Irish. A third of the signers of the Declaration of Independence were Irish or of Irish descent. The victory of the colonists in winning independence was energizing to the Irish in Ireland and around the world. Tiny Ireland, just forty miles off the coast of mighty England, became the second country after the American colonies to win its independence and start the dissolution of the modern British Empire.

A group of Irishmen put themselves deliberately in a death trap in Dublin in 1916 in the Easter Rebellion. Fifteen of the leaders were executed. They gave testimony that they knew they would be killed, but these deaths were *different*. Because—partly as a result of them—in time, the Irish stopped killing and being killed and gained power and influence around the world. These few deaths lit the time bomb that blew England out of six-sevenths of Ireland. The prototype of the collective unconscious of the Irish—a free man—became a perpetual reality. The hope and faith that truly makes all things possible had not died in Ireland. It was and is inextinguishable, and in time the energy of this hope will give the lie to anyone who says Ireland has no future, only the past happening over and over.

12 ☘ The Future of Ireland

Ireland can be a bridge between the Third World and the industrial democracies, and I intend to help make it happen.

JOHN FITZGERALD KENNEDY

IN AMERICA, even before the election of John F. Kennedy to the presidency—a dizzying achievement—the Wild Geese of Ireland had made their dreams come true in politics, the church, and the arts.

They made less progress in business until the fifties and sixties, but in the sixties and seventies their progress to the pinnacles of success in many fields was exponential.

John F. Kennedy was the breakthrough symbol for the Irish and Roman Catholics. He was very sensitive to this, and, partly because of this sensitivity, he invited me to visit him at the White House twice: once in his Oval Office; and then, two months before his death, in the living quarters on the third floor.

I was under no illusions as to why I had been invited to visit President Kennedy. As president of the world's biggest publishing company, Curtis, I could be important to the President by editorially supporting his legislative programs and, in his reelection campaign, the President himself. That was no vain hope, for after his assassination the *Saturday Evening Post* did switch support to a Democrat, Lyndon Johnson, as the only possible alternative to Barry Goldwater.

Nevertheless, I was surprised and flattered by President Kennedy's interest in me, in where my parents had been born, in what my brother and sisters did. When I realized that I'd been with the President twice as long as his press secretary, Pierre Salinger, predicted, I rose to leave. Kennedy said, "Just a minute. There's a friend of yours outside." He called to Miss Lincoln, his secretary, and in came Ollie Atkins, official White House photographer and also photographer for the *Post*. Ollie shot a half-dozen pictures, then we both knew I must leave. I stood up first, expressed my thanks, put out my hand. The President took it, shook it warmly, then put his left hand on my shoulder and said, "You know, it's nice to see an Irishman getting ahead in the business world."

When I laughed and looked startled, he said, "It's true. The Irish in America have done well in politics and the church, but not many have reached the top in business. My father was one of the first. Your success is a real accomplishment."

In retrospect, after reading the words of George Bernard Shaw in *John Bull's Other Island*, I thought of my own dreaming, dreaming, dreaming. As a youngster, I dreamed constantly of being an athletic hero, a dashing romantic ladies' man, a swashbuckling war hero, and later, after the war, I dreamed of becoming president of a glamorous company and a millionaire.

These were not disturbing or torturous dreams to me, though they worried my mother. She prayed that I would get a civil service job, even paid for me to go to Delehanty's to study to be a policeman. When I got my first job selling space for a magazine, she said, "Mother of God, what do you know about *real estate?*"

Later, a chauffeur-driven Cadillac was part of my fringe benefits as a rising executive of NBC. She looked at me with disbelief and suspicion when I picked her up for a drive. I believe she thought I had joined the Mob.

Why, I've asked myself in this search, did I get to be president or chief executive officer of not just one but three companies by the time I reached forty-five? Why did I leave a secure berth as president of the NBC Radio Network and executive vice-president of the whole National Broadcasting Company to enter a brand new business? Why did I leave a cushy job at Interpublic to become president of Curtis Publishing when I knew Curtis was ninety days from bankruptcy?

Why did I drop out of business, deciding on a new career as a writer at fifty years of age? And, particularly, why did I take on the quest for the Galloping Hogan, a quest consuming four years of time—time, my most precious and depleting asset?

Obviously because I'm a driven, inveterate dreamer, dreaming of a better world for those people and those places I love. I love the Irish people. I love Ireland. And I want much more for both. The Irish need heroes to replace those lost—Jack Kennedy, killed by an assassin, Charles Parnell, "killed" by jealous fellow countrymen.

The Galloping Hogan and Patrick Sarsfield are bona fide heroes. The Wild Geese of Ireland are being recognized as an extraordinary group of soldiers, political leaders, statesmen, writers, scholars, and teachers.

Definitive, incontrovertible evidence of who the Galloping Hogan was is, of course, beyond anyone's reach. I believe the Galloping Hogan was Michael Hogan. Readers, critics, and cynics can believe that, or favor one of the alternatives: he was captured and killed by the English at Cashel; he was killed in a battle with other Rapparees; there was more than one Hogan using the identity of the Galloping Hogan.

Of all the evidence of the Galloping Hogan, the most persuasive to me is that supplied by my mother who, in the Irish mode, heard it from her father, who heard it from his father, who heard it from his father, down through the centuries. Sarah Jane Hogan was the most honest woman I've ever known, incapable of guile or deceit. She and other family members believed the Galloping Hogan had gone to France. I proved that Michael Hogan had indeed gone to France, then to Portugal. I proved from both Portuguese military records and the records of the Irish Brigades that André Miguel Hogan was in the heroic mold of the Galloping Hogan.

And what of the other quest, for the quintessential spirit of the Irish? One final episode involving nine young Irishmen speaks volumes about the Irish, the Celtic spirit, the combination of daring, enterprise, irrepressibility and the willingness to take the consequences of their actions.

In Ireland in 1848, a group of young men were arrested, tried, and convicted of treason against Her Majesty, Queen Victoria. They had participated in an uprising known as the Young Ireland disorders.

As they stood before the bar to be sentenced, the judge asked if they had anything to say. The spokesman, Thomas Meagher, said, "My lord, this is our first offense, but not our last. If you will be easy with us this once, we promise on our word as gentlemen to do better next time. Sure, we won't be fools enough to get caught."

The enraged judge decreed that the defendants should be hanged, drawn, and quartered. Passionate and awesome protests caused Queen Victoria to commute the sentence to banishment for life and transportation to Australia.

In 1874 the queen was advised that Sir Charles Duffy, who had been elected prime minister of the province of Victoria in Australia, was the same young man who had taken part in an armed uprising. She indulged her queenly curiosity and demanded and received reports on the eight other treasonable Irishmen. This is what she found to her astonishment and chagrin.

Thomas Meagher became governor of Montana, and he was a general during the American Civil War.

Terrance McManus became a general in the United States Army.

Patrick Donahue became a general in the United States Army.

Richard O'Gorman became governor of Newfoundland.

Michael Ireland became attorney general of Australia.

Morris Lyene also became attorney general of Australia.

Thomas McGee became a member of Parliament in Canada and minister of agriculture.

John Mitchell became a writer and prominent politician in New York, fathering a son who became mayor of New York.

This episode is but a microcosm of the past tragedy of Ireland and the gain of the rest of the world during the oppression of Ireland. And what of the future?

I have more than just visited Ireland during the past five years of researching and writing this book. I have seen the astounding contrast of the Ireland of today and the Ireland of two decades, even one decade ago. I am convinced that Ireland is the emergent small country of Europe, with the best grazing land, the best protein diet, very much underpopulated (a blessing in some regards), a superabundance of water, an educated and lively younger generation, and growing pride in their survival with their ethnic characteristics and religion intact, after nearly a thousand years of oppression. Something wonderful is happening in Ireland. It is not yet a *solution* of the age-old problems of Northern Protestants and Catholics, but an *alleviation* of the problems at many levels. The major contributing factors to this alleviation are: the Women's Peace Movement; the revulsion at the cowardice and unhuman behavior of the terrorists who have killed and maimed women and children; the dwindling support of Americans for shadowy causes; the appeals of leading Americans of Irish descent for peaceful solutions; the astonishing improvement in living standards in the Irish Republic since 1922; and the weariness of the English, overwhelmed by their own problems, many of whom yearn to rid themselves of the financial, emotional, and physical burdens of Northern Ireland.

An extraordinary sign of this blessed alleviation was the relative mildness of the reaction to the visit of Queen Elizabeth to Northern Ireland during her Silver Jubilee. In another time and context there would have been extreme violence, death, and destruction. And, in the spring of 1978, a new mayor of Belfast was elected who is *not* a Unionist and is married to a Roman Catholic.

Miracles of patience, tolerance, and nonviolence cannot always be expected of the Irish, whose spirit is a volatile, heady mixture of intuitive, impulsive, and mystic forces, with a large overlay of fatalism and melancholy. But the Irish are learning that their ancestors, Celtic-related tribes, formed the first culture north of the Alps. The Celts were a distinct people around 800 B.C., the time of Homer, the first Greek Olympics, and the founding of Rome. As this epilogue is being written, major museums in America are featuring a collection of hundreds of exquisite pieces of Irish art and artifacts. Assuming the press coverage is commensurate with the significance of the exhibit, by the time the United States tour of the collection comes to an end, there will remain no skepticism or cynicism about what the tiny island of Ireland has contributed to Western Civilization from the sixth to the ninth centuries, during what is known as the Dark Ages.

When most of the Irish, North and South, Catholic and Protestant, comprehend what they are, and what they can be, the pace of alleviation of the country's problems will be accelerated. Then, permanent solutions will become possible.

It is important to note that Ireland is a new democracy in a world in which the trend has been running against democratic government. Ireland, though, has a very special place in the neutral ground between the industrial democracies and the Third World. Because Ireland has the respect and trust of the Third World countries, it could act as a bridge between these nations and the industrial democracies. The late President John F. Kennedy stated to Pierre Salinger that this was *his* hope for Ireland.

And dear patient reader, as I bid you farewell, this is my hope for you:

> May the road rise up to meet you.
> May the wind be always at your back.
> May the sun shine warm upon your face,
> The rains fall softly on your fields.
> And, until we meet again,
> May the Good Lord hold you in the palm of his hand.

Ancient Gaelic Farewell

Index